Barbara!
God's call is forever!

BLOOD, THE CURRENCY OF THE SPIRIT WORLD

BLOOD, THE CURRENCY OF THE SPIRIT WORLD

JACQUELINE TROUGHT

Copyright © 2013 by Jacqueline Trought
REVISED 2024
Blood, The Currency of the Spirit World
by Jacqueline Trought

ISBN 979-8-9907820-0-6 Softcover
ISBN 979-8-9907820-4-4 E-Book

All rights reserved solely by the author. The author guarantees all written contents are original with public domain graphics that do not knowledgeably infringe upon the legal rights of any other person or work. No part of this book may be reproduced in any form without the permission of the author or publisher except in cases of special quotations cited in critical articles or reviews.

Unless otherwise indicated, Bible quotations are taken from the King James Version of the Bible with edits.

Dedicated to my husband, Winston, whose insistence caused me to reach beyond and find the truth and wealth of the Presence of God. Also, to Mya, my granddaughter, who keeps inspiring my vision.

Contents

Dedication   v
Prologue   ix

1	Life is in the Blood	1
2	Smooth Deception	5
3	Religious Ties	14
4	A Time of Meditation	19
5	Blood for Redemption	31
6	Blood As a Covering	41
7	Blood Speaks	48
8	Spirit, Water, and Blood	56
9	God Speaks on the Abominations of Blood	65
10	Violations of Blood	74
11	Jesus' Blood	83
12	The Covenant of Marriage	94
13	Dabbling	107
14	Role of the Holy Spirit	115
15	Covenant Communion Passover	122
16	A Peak into the Future	141
17	Treasures Buried In Life's Adversities	150
18	Authority in Blood	157

19	Successful Prayers	163
20	The Business of Christ's Redemption	168
21	Then Comes the End	172

Prologue

The Earth is ruled by laws that govern every detail of its existence. For most, the sum is overwhelming, while others see the Earth as a giant that must be conquered. History has proven that the spirit world is the master controller of life and the use of blood has emerged as the currency that answers to it all.

With all its privileges and impossibilities, it becomes necessary to understand the formula by which Earth operates. Science, history, spiritual matters, and even the body points to the unique function of blood as the ultimate contributor to the laws of the spirit and of the Earth. Blood answers to every action of man, economically, judicially, and socially.

It is therefore wise to write on the parchment of life a story that aligns itself with the correct formula for success. Take the currency of the spirit to the vaults of the earth and open up the treasures that bring fulfillment. Write the story of peace and prosperity, leave an untainted legacy, and keep the heart dancing, using blood, the currency of the spirit world.

1

Life is in the Blood

*I have set before you life and death,
choose life
that both you and your children may live. Deuteronomy 30:19*

In the beginning, God created the Heavens and the Earth. Then God added light to the firmament and a host of decorations to brighten up the masterpiece He created. God stepped back admiringly, enjoying every detail of the magnificent garden He had prepared for His children. It was the perfection of holiness. Every bit of everything was connected to its support, and every support was in unison with God. Finally, it was time to add the main ingredient, so the Lord God formed man of the dust of the ground. Ahh, he was perfect; he was the very image of his Father.

Now, it was time for the kiss—the kiss of God. ...and God breathed into his nostrils the breath of life, and man became a living soul. (Genesis 2:7).

The breath entered his lungs and traveled to his heart. The breath warmed the heart, and the heart began beating, pounding its drum to the sound of the kiss. Blood heard the beat and came alive, bowed in reverence, and started a waltz with the cells. Blood began circulating throughout the body, carrying the happy news of life. The eyes popped open, the hands started clapping, the feet started moving, and the dance with life began. Blood is the carrier of life, and that life is the breath of God.

Blood is most intriguing, in that it carries both the physical and spiritual life of the body. To sustain physical life it needs nutrients, but to sustain spiritual life it needs breath. The same functions performed in the body are the same functions performed spiritually. Blood heals, it distinguishes, it defends, it determines the state of health, and it sacrifices itself for the body. After close examination, blood is the most important tissue of the body because it carries God; the breath of God. Blood speaks the language of the breath of God.

The bones of the body contain marrow, and the marrow churns out the stem cells that form the tissue we call blood. Blood is made from the cells which are tucked away inside the bone. But how did it all begin? In the womb, the cells multiply, then divide themselves into tissues. Next, the tissues multiply, then group themselves into organs. An amazing process. Just around the fifth week after conception, the heart, spinal cord, and brain will develop. Shortly after, the major blood vessels form, and the heart begins to pump blood with its first red blood cells.

How does the breath of God get inside the womb? Does God breathe each time conception occurs? The life of God is in the blood, which carries His breath. As long as the blood is alive, it carries the breath of God. If the cells of the father deposited in the womb are dead, the body rejects them, spits them out, and no life is formed. Life means it contains blood, it contains DNA, and it contains the breath of God. Those are the cells that multiply and form human life. The cells contain blood, and they contain DNA, but if they do not contain the breath of God, they cannot form life. Life is the gift of the Presence of the Lord woven into every cell of man, ready for existence on the Earth, ready to carry out the will of God, the Creator.

Every cell of the body must always surround itself with blood. Those cells that lose their connection with blood will eventually die. Blood never goes to sleep, never takes a break, and never gets tired because its functions are so important. Imagine being 100 years old and blood, circulating through the body, going as strong as the day of birth.

It collects nutrients from the intestines and distributes them from head to toe. Before returning to the heart, it assists in pulling out wastes and dumping them into the immune system. While it is busy moving up and down and to and fro, it is also balancing temperature and acidity, ensuring every tissue and organ is comfortable to carry out its normal function.

The red color of blood is attributed to little red cells suspended in the liquid, which are the main carriers of oxygen—the life of the blood. White cells swim alongside the red cells, and their role is to defend the body. The liquid portion of blood has a clear, watery look if all these cells—red cells, white cells, and other particles—are removed. The cells found inside the liquid have specific markers, and they identify the type of blood. Blood cells are some of the first to react to disease, and so the cells of the blood are often tested to determine health.

Man traces his identity through his blood. Just as his DNA points to his earthly father, so the breath of God points to his Heavenly Father. Man belongs to God. With the breath of God flowing through his arteries and veins, touching every cell, every tissue, every organ, it means every man is never out of touch with his Heavenly Father. Man cannot deny that there is something divine about himself, something greater than the world he can touch, see, smell, or taste. When he makes the connection with his earthly father, he stands to inherit earthly treasures. Also, as he hears the voice of his Heavenly Father, he knows he is born to love God and born for a divine purpose.

Man is the master of his world, complete with everything he needs to fulfill the purpose and pleasures for which he was created. At the center of this wonderful design, he is being touched by a bond so strong and so divine it makes him perfect. Indeed, man is the image of the Holy One, who has left His breath as proof of His love.

2

Smooth Deception

*I gave my heart to seek and search out wisdom
concerning all things done under Heaven.
This business has God given to the sons of men. Ecclesiastes 1:13*

Hell from beneath is moved for you to meet you at your coming. It stirs up the dead for you, even all the chief ones of the Earth.

Hell has risen up from her thrones all the kings of the nations. All of them shall speak and say, "Have you also become weak, as we are? Have you become like us?"

Your pomp and your pride have brought you down to the grave with the noise of your harps. The worm is spread under you, and worms cover you. How have you fallen from Heaven, O Lucifer, Son of the Morning? How are you cut down to the ground, you who made the nations weak?

For you said in your heart, "I will ascend into Heaven, and I will exalt my throne above the stars of God. I will sit also upon the Mount of the Congregation, in the sides of the North. I will ascend above the heights of the clouds, and I will be like the Most High God."

Yet you shall be brought down to Hell, to the deep parts of the pit. They that see you shall stare at you and consider you, saying, "Is this the man who made the Earth tremble? Is this the man who did shake kingdoms, that made the world as a wilderness, and destroyed cities? Is this the man that opened not the house of his prisoners?" (Isaiah 14:9–18).

The story above is about an angel named Lucifer. His heavenly name means Son of the Morning or Son of the Dawn; a gift to bear light for his heavenly Father. He was the perfection of beauty, full of wisdom, created to reflect the stunning features of the stones of fire. Imagine an angel whose dance with fire made the emblems sparkle and shine, lighting up the sky with fireworks that brought joy to all. That was Lucifer's role in Heaven, and he had an anointing to do it; he was perfect at bringing joy to all. Until... Lucifer covered the throne of God and ,along with one-third of the angels in Heaven, hatched a plan to overthrow God. The plot failed, and all the traitors were kicked out of Heaven. Everything that Lucifer possessed was tossed out with him—his beauty, his wisdom, the stones of fire—because everything he represented became corrupted.

Corruption raised those stones of fire to become his throne of Hell. The pompous one carved out a grave for himself and covered himself with the music of his harps. His corrupted heavenly wisdom made him weak. Weakness means he lost his ability to accomplish anything. He became frail, and puny, and wasted without the power that angels have to rule. No longer does he have access to heavenly power because he does not have access to Heaven. His only recourse is to set traps for man, take them prisoner, and steal man's God-given power and strength. Once he gets his claws on a prisoner, he locks that victim into a trap and buries the key in his graveyard. The only prisoners he can get his hands on are the children of God who live on the Earth. To steal their power, he must get them to violate their relationship with God. He uses the power of thought and words like a bullet to the head. Once the children are deceived into rejecting God, he wins.

In a roundabout way, Lucifer got his wish because after he was kicked out of Heaven, another spiritual kingdom was formed. He did not get God's throne, but he split God's treasures into pieces and has been stealing as much as he can since. He has been blatantly stealing the lives of the children of God, and if he doesn't have his way, he throws a fit. He throws a fit so often, he was given the name Satan, which means accuser. It is out of these stolen treasures that Lucifer has built his kingdom. Now, every person on the face of the Earth is registered either in the kingdom of God or the kingdom of Hell.

The world of the Heavens and Lucifer's kingdom of Hell are not easily understood by humans, except that we are given glimpses into the spiritual realm from time to time. What we do know is that the two spiritual kingdoms are distinctly set apart by right and wrong, good and evil.

The kingdom of God operates on laws that never change. The laws are like tiny nuggets on a treasure field. When a treasure is found, the finder can play finders keepers. If the finder decides to own that law, it has to be stuffed in the treasure bucket of the heart. The process is unfamiliar and a little clunky, but after the law becomes written on the table of the heart, it transforms the heart and makes it sweet and peaceful. For example, one of the laws states that man can touch God by talking with Him in prayer. That law is true, and every time man needs a miracle, he can reach out in reverence and receive miracles from the love of God.

The laws are to be desired more than gold—yes, than much fine gold. They are sweeter also than honey and the honeycomb. (Psalm 19:10).

On the other hand, the kingdom of darkness is marked by treason. Those who are trapped in the dungeon of darkness hate the games of lies, and betrayal, and cruelty that must be performed to stay in the loop. Lucifer has made a vow that the lake of everlasting fire, which was prepared for him and his angels, will be decorated with the souls of the weak and the broken. The goal is to drag men into evil and eventually into the lake of fire. The plan is loaded with deception and trickery: his rules are tailored specifically to bring death to the soul of man.

When God created Adam in the Garden of Eden, He gave Adam the unique gift of authority over all that was created. The Lord God specifically referred to the gift as dominion—which means subdue and rule the Earth. To ensure that every man knew what to do when he entered the Earth, God made it a law. Dominion is a legal, God-given gift, and every man has a right to it. God signed dominion into law before man was created, and when he arrived on Earth, those were the first words he heard. The first words man heard from the lips of God were, "Take dominion, subdue, and then you will be able to multiply successfully."

Like a great father, God gave His son everything he needed to be complete and to prosper. The power to destroy the evil that comes against man's soul was waiting when man arrived on Earth. Every man has the right, the permission, and the power to enjoy, to prosper, and to be at peace in the beautiful paradise of Earth. The sons of God who are placed on Earth were given the license to make their home a little heaven on Earth.

God came down in the cool of the day to fellowship with Adam and Eve in the garden of Eden. Like a good father would, He did not leave them to figure out their new home all by themselves. He knew the tree on which Lucifer perched, and without trying to scare Adam and Eve, He told them not to eat of its fruits. He could have said, "That is not a tree; it is a trap. That is not pleasure; it is a nightmare. A temporary high can create a permanent low." He could have said any of those words, words that would mean nothing if Adam and Eve did not trust Him.

One day, when God was not around, Lucifer visited Eve and had an interesting conversation with her. The evil one found out that he could stimulate the senses of the woman. He did not choose to share his ideas with the man because the man is practical. To get the man to disobey God, he would have to hand over something greater than the treasures God placed in the garden. To get the woman to chase the ghost of lies, all he had to do was paint a fantasy in her mind. The Devil caused the woman to believe that her life could be enhanced by simply bending an unimportant rule. As soon as he was satisfied that she was sufficiently duped, he dropped out of sight. Eve swallowed the lies without a shred of evidence.

Eve trusted the words she heard from God's enemy. To demonstrate her belief, she followed through on what she believed. Eve perhaps had no desire to taste the fruit of the forbidden tree. God, whom she and Adam loved, did not want her to eat of the tree, and that was enough. However, another opinion caused her to think twice. I wonder how long after the conversation with Lucifer, was Eve convinced to do that which she had never done before?

The Devil's words were, *You will become like gods.* (Genesis 3:5). What an exciting proposition. Is there any higher achievement? All that Eve possessed paled in the light of this offer. "I will offer you the ability to be like God; just do as I say." This may have been the sweetest lie to land on the ear of mankind. Amazingly, the same line is used today. "You will become famous, you will be rich, you will become successful;

just don't get caught." But, has anyone even come close to being a god, and doesn't everyone get caught?

An unholy exchange took place. There were fine prints, or in this case, an undertone to the Devil's words. If Eve obeyed his words, she would become his servant. As a servant, all she possessed would be turned over to him for ownership. What did Eve own? Land, lots of it. This is an understatement. Eve owned all of it. There is a difference between owning and possessing. Adam and Eve possessed the land—the whole Earth. Let's not forget the hidden spiritual value of the land: the dominion. Whoever has dominion is king of all. Dominion is the power to speak and watch the Earth hasten to obey the spoken word.

Another powerful treasure they possessed was the knowledge of God. Adam and Eve possessed infinite knowledge that was stolen in a moment of trickery. Holy, undefiled humans who fellowshipped with God daily (talk about holy communion) became empty and lost. In a heartbeat, just using words, Lucifer stole everything they owned and made them bankrupt. Now, he was emptied of everything that was pure and holy, and instead, filled with fear and mental pain.

The mental game that Lucifer played with the man and his wife is called sin. When Lucifer wins the game, he takes what he wants and leaves fear with his victim. The root of fear is shame, and shame feeds on disobedience. From that moment, Adam and Eve began to live their lives in shame because there was a breach of the state of purity and the safety of the perfect love of God. After sin was committed, it created the crack: a deep, wide, and ugly crack that separated Adam and Eve from all they had enjoyed and possessed. The ugliest part was that they did not know how to re-inherit or re-establish the bond needed to save them from this dreadful state.

Before they were tricked, Adam and Eve communicated daily with God on subjects of creation and the holiness of God's being—the questions we crave answers for. Who is God? Where does He come from? My granddaughter asked, "When is God's birthday?" She wanted to give Him birthday presents. This and more generated the serenity and sweetness that oozed between God and Adam—man enjoying God.

Those moments ruptured time. Man became lost in indescribable pleasure, serenading Love as He was designed to be reverenced, and Love responding by filling man with the power of His Spirit. The two became one, melded in thought and mind, allowing the exchange of fellowship to flow seamlessly without words, yet with potent understanding: intense joy and an unlimited exchange of ideas.

It is hard to imagine that the master of trickery and deception won the rights to Adam and Eve's minds. He stole the rights, and he took it all. Not only did he steal the rights to all their descendants, he also stole their souls. *Surely, I was sinful at birth, sinful from the time my mother conceived me.* (Psalm 51:5 NIV). He took the knowledge, the land, the dominion, and the fellowship, and he left man deprived and in a state of confusion.

The theory, "You will become like gods," was long forgotten in a tangled mess of abandonment. See, the evil one did not reveal the whole truth; he never does. His bill of goods is sold on false promises, and when he does not deliver, there is no reclaiming of lost value or clobbering the monster over the head for robbery. Man is left entirely on his own to sort out a godless existence and pending doom.

How did God respond to the sin of Adam and Eve? God sent His Son, Jesus, to the Earth to become the bearer (or the Christ) for the sins of Adam and all of Adam's children. In order to bear the sins, or in order to pay for their mistakes, Christ had to shed His blood. The plan was execution by hanging on a cross. Just like he did with Adam and Eve, Lucifer offered Jesus a deal. *Jesus, Son of God, bow down and worship me, reverence me, obey me, and I will give You all the kingdoms of this world and the glory of them. All the kingdoms of the world have been given to me and I give them to whomever I choose.* (Luke 4:5–7). If Jesus had accepted the offer, He would not have had to die for the sins of mankind.

If Jesus accepted the offer, it would have taken place through the exchange of words. Like a marriage, it would be a covenant made on the power of every single word. Words are programmed to perform. Words locked in the mind have some power, but they usually come alive when spoken or written. Intimate, spiritual, and business contracts are formed when words are spoken and written. Ideas are shaped when words are tossed and mingled in the pot of conversation, or arguments, or even rage. The pot is stirred by the heat of passion while the imagination cooks up a tasty brew. At the end of spending time together and sharing words, many deals have been born.

Jesus' bowing would have sealed the acceptance, after which Jesus would receive all that Lucifer had stolen from Adam and Eve in exchange for all the power He carried. Jesus could have the dominion, the possessions, and the land; He could have everything as long as He sealed the words by bowing. He who bows is the slave. The rest of the deceptive clause would read, 'Jesus never became Christ (Savior of the world), because He entered into an unholy alliance with Satan when He bowed and worshiped the enemy of God. He got the world and its glory, but He never reclaimed the lost souls of humanity. As a result, He was not able to go back to His Father, God. Of course He was ashamed, but the most damning result was that God lost complete fellowship with His children. Now, they are all subject to grotesque evils in their lives on Earth, and after death, they enter the flames of eternal Hell.' But Jesus was not swayed by the cunning lies of evil. Jesus knows the Devil cannot deliver on any promise. He is just a liar; in fact, Lucifer is the Father of Lies.

No need to belabor the point that the plot continues. Everyone who flees the camp of evil to serve the living God will come face-to-face with the decision to accept the subtle offer of selling their soul. Sweet offers are made to satisfy the cravings of the heart when the soul is in a state of anxiety. The heart, in its desperation, swallows the pill of lies before it opens its eyes. The offer to sell the soul is a death trap. Of course, the Devil will lie, but even a fool knows when he hears a lie.

The Devil cannot deliver. The bottom line is that the Devil has never stopped hunting prey, and the snake charm of his subtle, lying offers will be dancing on the table to hypnotize the mind. But God never leaves His children. In the midst of the hoopla, the Presence of God is standing by with the power to turn off the switch so His children can turn their backs on evil, and wait for the salvation of God.

It does bring up the question, with the intensity of fellowship experienced between Adam, Eve, and God, and their subsequent failure, who then can qualify for an undefiled relationship with this holy God? I am glad you asked. Let's sigh with relief for the pure and precious blood of Jesus Christ, Son of the living God.

Religious Ties

Consider and hear me, O Lord my God.
Enlighten mine eyes, lest I sleep the sleep of death. Psalm 13:3

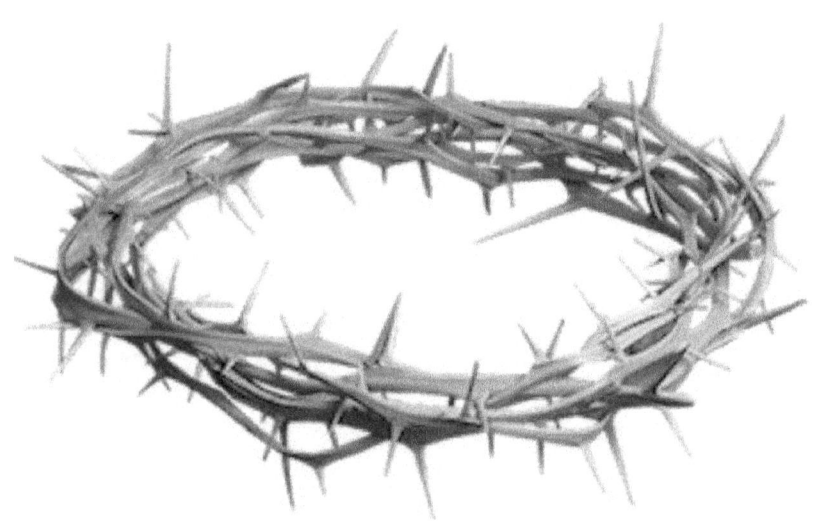

Man has run the gamut of religion. If it is out there, someone is going to find it. If it does not exist and someone envisions it, bet your bottom dollar it will be created. Why? Man was created to worship, and if he does not find God, it is certain that he will create a god for himself.

Some of us have accepted the concept that if there is a God, a creator, He must be bigger and greater than our minds would allow us to perceive. Therefore, our faith rests in the revelation He has handed to us. The mystery that surrounds His omniscience, omnipresence, and omnipotence will suffice, because anything less reduces Him to our limitations. Our search is diligent and unstoppable. Our reverence is deep. Our explanation is beyond words, so we humbly express ourselves in steadfast faith.

Still, others have placed their faith in God through humans or objects. This faith seeks to connect with God through an object or someone that can be seen. The connection is indirect yet sincere, and the object becomes a medium of the symbol of God. An individual will touch a cross at the end of a necklace and gain a sense of peace that somehow God is there through that cross. Masses of people attend church just to keep alive their connection with God. This is a step of precaution without any real connection. There is no one-on-one communication between their lives and God. Therefore, this life is easily swayed to believe anything, because true knowledge is missing.

Then, there are religions that have created and fashioned gods they can touch, and see, and handle. If one cannot see it, taste it, touch it, or smell it, the limited mind says it cannot exist. This creation is rooted in the need to heal broken emotions since the emotions were damaged by horrific images, or hands that brought pain, or by touch that damaged the soul. A god that is visible makes absolute sense to the mind whose intellect is trained to maneuver and conquer a physical world. Yet, it must ignore the unspoken law that a god must be greater than its followers. This created god has one small flaw that cannot be overlooked: this god is smaller and weaker than its creation. It has no power to bestow gifts on the one who serves it, because the creation is greater than the god.

Other religious forms trust in self to analyze the maze of life and to find inner peace. Again, this belief carries the idea that if the concept cannot be explained, if it leaves gaps of unanswered questions or unsuitable definitions, then it lacks the qualifications to satisfy complete submission and worship. The worshiper therefore creates a god rooted in self. Since self cannot provide fulfillment, this religion leads to the endless search for more and eventually skews rights and wrongs, truths and lies. Grasping for solutions, it creates crafty answers to define the unexplainable. Self becomes the all-important one, a creator of ideas, then philosophy, then a kingdom. With that in hand, self seeks to be worshiped, believing it is god because it has become a master of control. As pride ties the knot with control, self cries out, "I am a god, worship me."

There is more. Some have followed blood rituals and rites that qualify them to increase and rise above the status quo while achieving the unthinkable. These rituals and rites become their power source. To keep increasing power, the seeker must continue making those religious sacrifices as more rituals lead to more power. While it is true that those who partner with the spirit world are granted degrees of power, the power granted is only a clever scheme of continuous manipulation. Shrewd manipulation becomes the power that flirts with the senses and bestows an attitude of greatness. This then becomes the milestone, the marker that ushers the seeker beyond, and greatness becomes godliness.

It is not easy to fathom each man's notion of God, as all these religious ties are simply man's search for the true and living God. Even those who congregate to honor the lord of a common faith differ in understanding and knowledge of the god they serve. But we must explore this last facet of another type of religion. There are those who worship Lucifer as god. Mind-blowing information exists on the doctrine and the rituals performed by these followers, but most intriguing are their deep expressions of trust. Those who turn their hearts to Lucifer seek to pacify their need for revenge on life, but mostly their revenge on God. Yet, no man does surgery on his own heart. A man whose heart needs fixing entrusts his life to a surgeon who is qualified to repair it; he does not plunge a knife in, hoping to cut out the damaged areas. Revenge is the fool's method of victory but the sure path to increasing pain. Lucifer offers comfort for the pain he caused by handing a sword to his victim to finish the damage he started. To be knighted with the sword of Lucifer means the victim must consciously dedicate their time and soul to the beast.

At its foundation, all religion obligates its followers to some form of worship. All religions require due diligence, and in return there is a gift, a treasure of value that its subjects seek. The exchange between god and man, and the requirements of the exchange, take matters to levels unimaginable. There are practices that require the killing of animals, or piercings and markings on the body, or children to be offered by fire to the gods. All these sacrifices are given in exchange for a great life here on Earth. We also cannot forget the ultimate sacrifice of one's own life, in the name of religion, in exchange for a better life in the hereafter.

You shall not let any of your children pass through the fire to Molech, neither shall you profane the Name of Your God: I am the LORD. (Leviticus 18:2).

And they caused their sons and their daughters to pass through the fire and used divination and enchantments and sold themselves to do evil in the sight of the LORD, to provoke Him to anger. (2 Kings 17:17).

He made his son pass through the fire and observed times and used enchantments and dealt with familiar spirits and wizards. He did much wickedness in the sight of the LORD to provoke Him to anger. (2 Kings 21:6).

Religious requirements are strange. The measures humans have taken to attain the dream of life as we know it have left the planet in mourning. Beyond the devastation wreaked are the lies, cover-ups, hatred, wars, and division that have been generated; yet the promise was to attain greater and better things. Is this a revelatory moment to ask, "If my achievement is indeed a good thing, why is my soul in such agony and shame?"

For those of us who have not been rendered callous by the deeds and promises of an unfulfilling religion, the soul still waits for truth. Somewhere out there exists a God who can rectify and restore, who can truly make crooked places straight, who can repair the breach, and who can make all things work together for good if we choose to love Him. By its definition, religion is the way that is right where the end is not destruction. That is the reason God never offers Himself to man as religion; God offers Himself as a Father. Father means there is a personal covenant between God and His children, and the treasures of love that He offers will heal and perfect the heart.

In keeping with the law of the Spirit, God must absolutely be beyond what the mind can perceive and greater than man's explanation. A childlike faith to seek out the truth of God, bears the solution to true peace and prosperity. But how can man truly know God? It is belief that leads to religion. Can knowledge be trusted to yield truth?

The secrets of life are hidden to those who are proud in spirit, but a broken and humble heart God will not refuse. (Psalm 51:17).

The true and living God waits to nurture and love His children, and those who seek to find Him, He will never turn away.

4

A Time of Meditation

When wisdom enters your heart, and knowledge is pleasant to your soul, discretion will preserve you and understanding will keep you. Proverbs 2:10

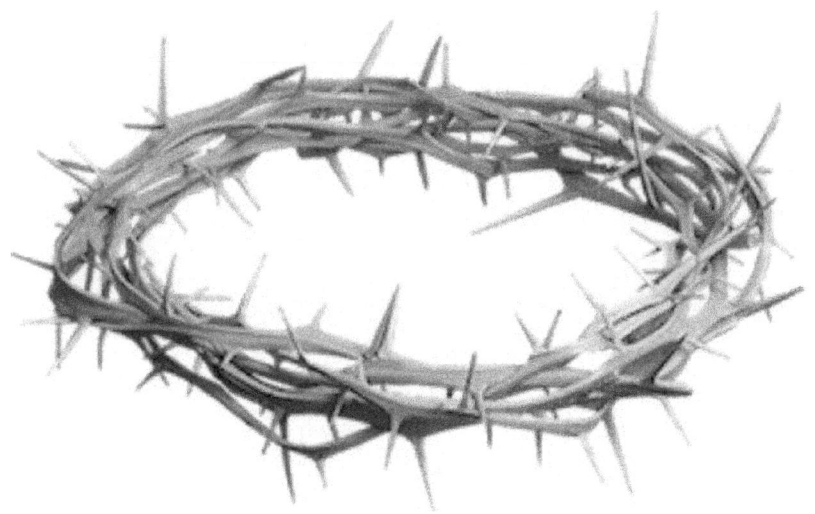

Now, this is the story of the birth of Jesus Christ. His mother, Mary, was engaged to Joseph, but before they came together, she was found with child of the Holy Ghost. Joseph, her husband, being a just man and not willing to make her a public example, began planning to put her away privately. But while he thought on these things, behold, the angel of the Lord appeared to him in a dream, saying, "Joseph, son of David, do not be afraid to take Mary as your wife, because that which is conceived in her is of the Holy Ghost. She shall bring forth a son, and you shall call His name JESUS, for He shall save His people from their sins." Now all this was done that it might be fulfilled which was spoken of the Lord by the prophet, saying, "Behold, a virgin shall be with child, and shall bring forth a son, and they shall call His name *Emmanuel*, which, being interpreted is, *God with us*." Then Joseph, being raised from sleep, did as the angel of the Lord told him and took Mary as his wife. (Matthew 1:18–24).

And in the sixth month, the angel Gabriel was sent from God to a city of Galilee named Nazareth, to a virgin engaged to a man whose name was Joseph, of the house of David. The virgin's name was Mary. The angel came to her and said, "Hail, you that are highly favored, the Lord is with you; blessed are you among women." When she saw him, she was troubled by his saying and wondered why he would greet her with those words. And the angel said unto her, "Fear not, Mary, for you have found favor with God. Behold, you shall conceive in your womb and bring forth a son, and shall call His name Jesus. He shall be great and shall be called the Son of the Highest, and the Lord God shall give unto Him the throne of His father David. He shall reign over the house of Jacob forever, and of His kingdom there shall be no end." Then said Mary to the angel, "How shall this be, seeing I know not a man?" And the angel answered, "The Holy Ghost shall come upon you, and the power of the Highest shall overshadow you; therefore, that holy thing which will be born of you shall be called the Son of God.

And behold, your cousin Elisabeth has also conceived a son in her old age. This is the sixth month with her who was called barren, for with God nothing shall be impossible." And Mary said, "Behold the handmaid of the Lord; be it unto me according to your word." And the angel departed from her. (Luke 1:26–38).

For unto us a child is born, unto us a son is given. The government shall be upon His shoulder, and His name shall be called Wonderful, Counselor, The Mighty God, The Everlasting Father, The Prince of Peace. Of the increase of His government and peace there shall be no end, upon the throne of David and upon His kingdom, to order it and to establish it with judgment and with justice from henceforth even forever. The zeal of the LORD of Hosts will perform this. (Isaiah 9:6–7).

For God so loved the world that He gave His only begotten Son, that whosoever believes in Him will not perish but have everlasting life. For God sent His Son into the world, not to condemn the world, but that the world through His Son might be saved. (John 3:16–17).

Come unto Me, all you who labor and are heavy laden, and I will give you rest. Take My yoke upon you, and learn of Me, for I am meek and lowly in heart, and you shall find rest unto your souls. For My yoke is easy, and My burden is light. (Matthew 11:28–30).

Repent and be converted, that your sins may be blotted out when the times of refreshing shall come from the Presence of the Lord. And He shall send Jesus Christ, who was preached unto you, whom Heaven must receive until the times of restitution of all things, which God has spoken by the mouth of all His holy prophets since the world began. For Moses truly said unto the fathers, "God will raise up a prophet like me unto you, from among your brethren. All things whatsoever He shall say unto you, be careful to hear Him." (Acts 3:19–22).

But this is a people plundered and looted, all of them trapped in holes or imprisoned in dungeons. They have become plunder with no one to rescue them, and loot with no one saying, "Give it back!" Who among you will pay attention to this? Let him listen and obey because the time is coming. (Isaiah 42:22–23).

Surely, He has borne our grief and carried our sorrows; yet we did esteem Him stricken, smitten of God, and afflicted. But He was wounded for our transgressions; He was bruised for our iniquities; the chastisement of our peace was upon Him, and with His stripes we are healed. All we like sheep have gone astray, we have turned everyone to his own way, and the LORD has laid on Christ the iniquity of us all. (Isaiah 53:4–6).

He was oppressed, and He was afflicted, yet He opened not His mouth. He is brought as a lamb to the slaughter, and as a sheep before her shearer is dumb, so He opened not His mouth. He was taken from prison and from judgment, and who shall declare His generation? For He was cut off out of the land of the living; for the transgression of My people was He stricken. And He made His grave with the wicked and with the rich in His death. Because He had done no violence, neither was there any deceit in His mouth, it pleased the Lord to bruise Christ and to put Him to grief. When God shall make His Son's soul an offering for sin, He shall see His seed, He shall prolong His days, and the pleasure of the Lord shall prosper in His hand. God shall see the travail of His Son's soul and shall be satisfied, because by the knowledge Christ gained in suffering, God's righteous servant shall justify (heal) many: for He shall bear their iniquities. Therefore, God will divide Christ a portion with the great, and Christ shall divide the spoil with the strong because He has poured out His soul unto death, He was numbered with the transgressors, He bore the sin of many, and He made intercession for the transgressors. (Isaiah 53:7–12).

Christ, by Himself, took our sins into His own body on the cross so that we, being dead to sins, should live unto righteousness. By whose stripes we were healed. For we were as sheep going astray, but are now returned unto the Shepherd and Bishop of our souls. (1 Peter 2:24–25).

Then said Jesus unto His disciples, "If any man will come after Me, let him deny himself, take up his cross, and follow Me." (Matthew 16:24).

I am not ashamed of the gospel of Christ, for it is the power of God unto salvation to everyone who believes, to the Jew first, and also to the Greek. For in the gospel, the righteous heart of God is revealed, and through the beauty of this knowledge, we rise from faith to faith. As it is written, 'The just shall live by faith.' (Romans 1:16–17).

Blessed are your eyes for they see, and your ears for they hear. (Matthew 13:16).

For this purpose the Son of God revealed Himself to you, that He might destroy the works of the Devil. (1 John 3:8).

Every time I think about this, I am filled with hope. It is of the LORD's mercies that we are not consumed; it is because His compassion never fails. They are new every morning and great is God's faithfulness. "The Lord is my portion," says my soul; "therefore, I will hope in Him. The Lord is good to those who wait for Him, to the soul that seeks Him. It is good that a man should both hope and quietly wait for the salvation of the Lord." (Lamentations 3:21–26).

The wilderness and the solitary place shall be glad, and the desert shall rejoice and blossom as the rose. It shall blossom abundantly and rejoice with joy and singing. The glory of Lebanon shall be given unto it, the excellence of Carmel and Sharon; they shall see the glory of the Lord and the excellence of our God. Strengthen your weak hands, and steady those feeble knees. Say to them who are of a fearful heart, "Be strong! Fear not! Behold, your God will come with vengeance; God will come and make things right; He will come and save you." (Isaiah 35:1–4).

Wisdom is the principal thing; therefore, get wisdom, and while you are searching for everything in life, get understanding. Exalt her, and she shall promote you. She shall bring you honor when you embrace her. She shall give to your head an ornament of grace; a crown of glory shall she hand to you. (Proverbs 4:7–9).

Can a woman forget her sucking child, that she should not have compassion on the son of her womb? Yes, she may forget, yet I will not forget you. Behold, I have graven (tattooed) you on the palms of My hands; your walls are continually before Me. (Isaiah 49:15–16).

Have you not known? Have you not heard that the Everlasting God, the Lord, the Creator of the ends of the Earth, faints not, neither is weary? There is no searching of His understanding. He gives power to the faint, and to them who have no might He increases strength. Even the youths shall faint and be weary, and the young men shall utterly fall. But they that wait upon the Lord shall renew their strength; they shall mount up with wings as eagles, they shall run and not be weary, and they shall walk and not faint. (Isaiah 40:28–31).

Heal me, O Lord, and I will be healed; save me, and I will be saved, for You are my praise. (Jeremiah 17:14).

"It is easier for a camel to go through the eye of a needle than for a rich man to enter into the kingdom of God." When Jesus' disciples heard it, they were exceedingly amazed: "Who then can be saved?" But

Jesus beheld them and said unto them, "With men this is impossible, but with God all things are possible." (Matthew 19:24–26).

I am the door; by Me if any man enters in, he shall be saved and will go in and out and find pasture. The thief only comes to steal, to kill, and to destroy. I AM come that you might have life and that you might have life in its abundance. I AM the good Shepherd, and the good Shepherd gives His life for the sheep. (John 10:9–11).

I AM the good Shepherd, I know My sheep, and My sheep know Me. As the Father knows Me, even so I know the Father, and I lay down My life for the sheep. (John 10:14–15).

My sheep hear My voice, I know them, and they follow Me. I give them eternal life and they shall never perish, neither shall any man pluck them out of My hand. My Father who gave them to Me, is greater than all, and no man is able to pluck them out of My Father's hand. (John 10:27–29).

I love the Lord, because He has heard my voice and my supplications. Because He has inclined His ear unto me (turned His attention to listen to me), therefore will I call upon Him as long as I live. The sorrows of death passed all around me, and the pains of Hell got a hold of me: I found trouble and sorrow. Then I called upon the Name of the Lord, "O Lord, I beseech You, untie my soul from Hell." Gracious is the Lord, and righteous. Yes, our God is merciful, the Lord preserves the simple. I was brought low, and He helped me. Return unto your rest, O my soul, for the Lord has dealt bountifully with you. For God has delivered my soul from death, my eyes from tears, and my feet from falling. (Psalm 116:1–8).

Be it known unto you all, and to all the people of Israel, that by the Name of Jesus Christ of Nazareth, whom you crucified, whom God raised from the dead, even by Him does this man stand here before you whole. This is the stone which the builders rejected, which has become the head of the corner. Neither is there salvation in any other, for there is no other name under Heaven given among men whereby we must be saved. (Acts 4:10–12).

He brought them out of the prison and said, "Sirs, what must I do to be saved?" And they said, "Believe on the Lord Jesus Christ, and you shall be saved, and your house." And they spoke to him the Word of the Lord and to all who were in his house. And he took them the same hour of the night and washed their stripes and was baptized, he and all his house. (Acts 16:30–33).

For when we were yet without strength, in due time Christ died for the ungodly. For scarcely for a righteous man will one die, yet peradventure for a good man some would even dare to die. But God commends His love toward us, in that, while we were yet sinners, Christ died for us. Much more then, being now made just-as-if we never sinned by Christ's blood, we shall be saved from God's wrath through Christ. For if, when we were enemies of God, we were purchased from sin and restored to God by the death of His Son, much more now, since we have been restored to fellowship with God, we shall be saved by Christ's life. And not only so, but we also joy in God through our Lord Jesus Christ, by whom we have now received access to God's Presence. This is what happened: sin was introduced into the world by one man, then death came because of sin. So, death passed over all men because all men were born into sin. Now, sin was already in the world when God gave Moses the set of rules to avoid sin. So, God did not count sin against those who did not receive those laws. Even though God did not hold men's sins against them, it did not mean that they escaped the devastation of sin. As a result, death reigned from Adam to Moses even over people who chose to keep themselves pure and free from sin. (Romans 5:6–14).

Just as sin entered the world through one man, and death entered through sin, so death came upon all people because all have sinned. Let us be clear, sin was in the world before the law was given, but sin is not charged against anyone's account where there is no law. (Romans 5:12).

Now, there is a gift that God gave to one man. A man who is as special as Adam in God's eyes, but the gift is not like the sin of Adam. Many died by the sin of Adam, but now because of God's grace—and the gift that came by the grace of that One Man, Jesus Christ—life will overflow to many! Also, the gift of God cannot be compared with the results of one man's sin. Judgment followed one sin and brought condemnation, but the gift followed many sins and brought complete wholeness. Death ruled people's lives because of the sin of one man; how much more will the divine bliss of life given by the tender grace of God, how much more will that life reign in us because of the one man, Christ Jesus. Consequently, just as one trespass resulted in condemnation for all people, so also one righteous act results in acquittal and life for all people. For just as through the disobedience of one man many were made sinners, so also through the obedience of one man, many will be made righteous. The law was brought in so that sin might be exposed for the evil and devastation it brings. And where sin increased, grace increased even more: so that, just as sin reigned and brought death with it, so also grace might reign through doing the right thing to bring eternal life through Jesus Christ our Lord. (Romans 5:12–20, NIV).

Your Word have I hid in my heart, that I might not sin against You. (Psalm 119:11).

What is that saying? The Word of God is near you; it is in your mouth and in your heart. You know it; it is the Word of Faith that we preach. That is why, if you will confess with your mouth the Lord Jesus Christ and will believe in your heart that God has raised Him from the dead, you will be saved. For when a man believes anything with his heart, he will chase it down, and he will do it. Same with the mouth; whatever he believes, he will speak it until it becomes his salvation. For the scripture says, "Whosoever believes on Jesus Christ shall not be ashamed, and there is no difference between the Jew or the Greek. Jesus Christ is the same Lord over us all, and He is rich unto all that call upon Him. For whosoever shall call upon the Name of the Lord shall be saved. (Romans 10:8–13).

Then Jonah prayed unto the Lord his God out of the fish's belly and said, "I became so stressed with pain and suffering, that I cried unto the Lord, and He heard me. Out of the belly of Hell I cried, and You, God, heard my voice. For You have cast me into the deep in the midst of the seas, and the floods covered me. All Your billows and Your waves passed over me." Then I said, "I am cast out of God's sight, yet I will look again toward His holy temple. The waters continued to cover me, even to my soul. The depth of darkness closed in around me, while the weeds of trouble wrapped themselves around my head. I sank down to the bottom of the mountains; the Earth with her bars was around me everywhere. Yet, God, You found me; You brought up my life from corruption, O Lord, My God. When my soul fainted within me, I remembered the Lord and my prayer came in unto You, into Your holy temple. They that observe lying vanities forsake their own mercy. But I will sacrifice unto You with the voice of thanksgiving; I will pay that which I have vowed. Salvation is of the Lord." And the Lord spoke to the fish, and it vomited out Jonah upon the dry land. (Jonah 2).

Order my steps in Your Word, and let not any iniquity have dominion over me. (Psalm 119:133).

Being confident of this very thing, that He who has begun a good work in you will perform it until the day of Jesus Christ. (Philippians 1:6).

Grace be to you, and peace, from God our Father, and from the Lord Jesus Christ. Blessed be the God and Father of our Lord Jesus Christ, who has blessed us with all spiritual blessings in heavenly places in Christ. According as He has chosen us in Him before the foundation of the world, that we should be holy and without blame before Him in love. (Ephesians 1:2-4).

Long before we came to the Earth, God predestined us to become adopted by Jesus Christ to Himself. That adoption was written in God's will with pleasure; it brought praise and glory to the grace of God that He found the way, through adoption, to make us accepted in His beloved family. (Ephesians 1:5-6)

To seal the adoption, Christ paid a ransom for us. The price of the ransom was His blood. Now that all sins have been paid, we all have been forgiven—that is how rich grace is. Included in this rich and boundless grace, God has included all wisdom so that we do not mentally sentence ourselves to doom. God also made known to us the hidden secrets and mysteries of His will. The will contains all that He has purposed to do, which brings Him pleasure. God sees into the future; He looks ahead to a time when He will gather all His chosen who are adopted in Christ to Himself, whether they are in Heaven or in the Earth. Those who have accepted Christ have obtained an inheritance and are made eligible because God's will only works according to the laws which He has set. This inheritance is a special reward for those who trusted in Christ, even before they had any confirmation around them to prove the evidence of Christ. They trusted after they heard the Word of Truth, which became good news to their ears, the gospel of salvation. And once they believed in Christ, they were sealed with that Holy Spirit of Promise. (Ephesians 1:7-13).

And the God of peace shall bruise Satan under your feet shortly. The grace of our Lord Jesus Christ be with you. Amen. (Romans 16:20).

"As for Me, this is My covenant with them," says the LORD; "My spirit that is upon you and My Words which I have put in your mouth, shall not depart out of your mouth, nor out of the mouth of your children, nor out of the mouth of your children's children, from now until forever," says the LORD. (Isaiah 59:21).

Forever, O LORD, Your Word is settled in Heaven. (Psalm 119:89).

Amen.

5

Blood for Redemption

Blood is the only currency accepted in the heavenly realm.

At the fall of Adam and Eve, God introduced a shocking principle called redemption. Redemption means paying the asking price to reclaim that which is extremely valuable. In this case, the asking price on the auction block was blood, and God shed the blood of an animal to redeem Adam and his wife, then used its skin to cover their nakedness. As we observe the never-changing pattern of God, we can guess that the animal chosen for the sacrifice was a lamb. Imagine being chosen as the sacrifice for someone else's failure. The strange thing about a lamb is that it goes willingly to the slaughter. It does not fight; it does not resist the knife, as if lambs were born to be sacrifices for man's failures.

In order for God to continue visiting, and talking, and having fun with Adam and Eve, they had to be pardoned from their sins. The shedding of blood was given for the pardon of sins. Later, Noah appeased God's heart with a sweet-smelling savor of blood offerings when the episode of the ark was ended (Genesis 8). Further on in the Levitical writings, as God established the laws for His own nation, He commanded them to bring burnt offerings, fellowship offerings, sin offerings, and guilt offerings, all from the shedding of blood. Various scriptures state that when blood is shed, then burned by fire as an offering to God, it pleases the Lord.

The children of Israel were Egyptian slaves for over four hundred years, and God decided to end the atrocity. He said to His servant, Moses, *I have heard the cry of My children, and I AM come down to help them.* (Exodus 3:7). Well, did God lift a finger? No, instead, He gave specific instructions; He gave them a process. Every time God spoke, and Moses followed His instructions, it destroyed the power of Egypt. Then came the moment when God was ready to completely destroy the cruelty of slavery, and God required the shedding of blood.

When blood is shed on the Earth, it activates and deactivates bondages in the Heavens. When blood is shed as a sacrifice to a spiritual being, it moves the spirit world to reinforce or to shatter chains of bondage. The very night the children of Israel sacrificed their lambs to God, the shackles of slavery were cast off from them. On the flip side of that coin, their obedience to the sacrifice of God activated the death of the firstborn of the Egyptians.

Imagine hundreds of thousands of people living under the bondage of the whip, their wounds and bandages constantly being ripped open by the sting of the lash. Imagine waking up in fear, waiting for the familiar sounds of heartbreaking screams, knowing that the day would be full of pain. Imagine living in slavery with no power to change the evil. Logically, there must have been plots of escape, plans to overthrow the government, rebellion, and boycott. Moses himself offered his services by killing an Egyptian whom he thought wronged an Israelite, but nothing budged. In fact, life only got harder for the oppressed and the wounded. Then came the day of salvation; God was ready, and the people were ready. If God had broken the bondage without showing the people His power, they would have had no confidence in Him. God had to teach the people to listen to His words and to trust them. He taught them to trust Him by breaking the spirit of Pharaoh, and every lesson He taught destroyed the gods of Egypt. On the day God broke the bondage, the people were in total agreement with God, and God gave them specific instructions to offer a blood sacrifice.

Let's reason this out. An entire nation was in bondage, suffering cruelty at the hands of merciless taskmasters. For 430 years they kept crying to the God they served, and though they received no answer, they cried, nonetheless. Then God answered their desperation by giving instructions on the shedding of blood. The answer was so potent, it relieved more than half a million men (not counting wives or children) of the mental, emotional, and physical bondage that suffocated generations and engraved itself on their culture. It transformed slaves into soldiers, servants into leaders, and instruction-takers into nation-builders.

Sin brings death to the soul of man. In fact, sin is the thief of a great life because the wage of sin is death. The children were locked in the sin of slavery, and the only joy they had was the relief of death. God walks into the camp with His tried-and-true principle of redemption: *I am purchasing you from the hands of Pharaoh.* That purchase could not have taken place until the people trusted God to become their deliverer. Now that everyone was in agreement, it was time to pay the price, to offer the sacrifice that would activate the release. Shed blood was the satisfactory price, offered and accepted, that released the spiritual bondage and physical chains of Israel.

It seems logical that the blood of the lambs that were slaughtered should have been offered to Pharaoh, since he cracked the whip of slavery. But Pharaoh was only the poster boy for the god of evil, and because he was being used by evil, he was tied into a greater level of bondage than the Israelites. One can only imagine the nightmares and misery of a man who rules by the power of darkness.

The most powerful aspect of redemption is the one to whom the blood is given. Shed blood is offered to the master who requests the sacrifice. Each time blood is shed to satisfy spiritual rituals, it becomes payment to a specific master. Sacrificing a life is a spiritual payment when it is offered to the unseen. Spiritual payments are presented to God or the Devil, then the blood that is spilled marks the life of the one who offers the sacrifice. The master who receives the sacrifice claims ownership of the one who offers the sacrifice.

Technically, sinners are servants of the Devil. Well, technically. He owns sinners because he uses them to work for him. To be freed from that bondage or to be in right standing with God would necessitate a purchase of the sinner from the owner. In our given system of trade, every purchase receives an equal exchange; owners walk away from the bargaining table with substances of equal value. According to Earth's system of trade, the shed blood of Jesus Christ should be offered to the Devil as payment for the sin of mankind. However, the holy blood of Jesus Christ, shed for the pardon of sins, is not given to the Devil as an exchange for a life.

Without question, the Devil cannot accept the purity of the holy blood of Christ, or he would be made pure. Anyone who says *Yes*, to the shed blood of Christ is instantly freed from the haunting disease of darkness. The spirit world operates on a different frequency than the Earth as there is no trade or exchange of goods for a price. Trade deals are governed by levels of power. The one with the greatest purchasing power claims the goods, and there are no negotiations or bargaining contracts. The marker on the blood of Christ denotes its power, and as it is shed, it frees the prisoner from the chains of evil. The blood itself unlocks the hold of bondage and releases the sinner from its dungeon. That is the purchasing power of the blood of Christ.

When anyone, the whosoever, did whatever (except blasphemy against the Holy Ghost), upon repentance, asks for the pardon that comes with the shed blood of Jesus Christ, the blood of Christ instantly untangles that life from sin. This blood purifies the heart and mind and releases the soul from the grip of any demonic bondage. The blood of Christ covers the life for which it was shed with protection, and supernaturally establishes new ownership. That is the paid-for redemptive plan of Jesus Christ.

The asking becomes the crux of the matter because release does require *free will*. In its state of decay and death, where the soul has lost its favor with God, a sincere cry activates the compassion of the heart of Jesus Christ. With loving intercession, Jesus turns to His Father and petitions the heart of God for the sprinkling of His shed blood from the throne.

Every request is honored. God releases the grace of healing with the blood to cover the soul, frees it from the bondage of sin, and restores it to life and health in God. Now, we can see that redemption is not a system of exchange but rather a freeing of the soul from the shackles of death. Evil has to needle its way into the heart of man, and therefore ownership is not lawfully established, nor is it permanent. The bondage and the label, Sinner, were deeded by trickery. Evil uses smooth deception to buy unsuspecting souls who are gullible and naïve to the dangers of sin. It steals souls in innocence, covers them with bitterness, bottles them, and flaunts the package before their faces. The gullible chase the bottle, hoping to become whole, only to find themselves in a slippery hole with no end. Sin does know how to feed the appetite, and it serves up an irresistible brew, but the blood of Christ is greater than bondage.

At the age of accountability, when mankind consciously begins to reject God and choose sin, we establish the team on which we serve. Life screams relentlessly at the heart, demanding that each man produce treasures from the potential placed inside. The demand places pressure on the mind creating a mental drain which is interpreted as need. Sliding down the slippery slope of need, we sell our souls to the Devil when blood is shed to satisfy the gods of darkness, establish control, or protection. The misguided call to satisfy need becomes a rope that pulls us deeper and deeper into sin.

Escape to the kingdom of the living God is also confirmed by blood, but that blood is already shed. To enter into the safety and protection of Almighty God, one must believe in and trust the blood that was shed by Jesus Christ on Calvary. God never turns anyone away, and all who cry out for His covering, like the children of Israel, experience God's saving grace. That is the born-again experience. From whatever angle we take it, bloodshed answers to a higher power.

Man knows that to take life to another level, sacrifices must be made. When sacrifices are given in the form of blood, man is no longer tampering with mere humanity; he is meddling with spiritual beings. Blood from animals or humans, offered as a sacrifice to the Devil, awakens the beasts of Hell and its master to cement their unrestricted control over the lives involved. Once that blood enters the throne of Hell, it unleashes and activates ruthless demons filled with venomous desires to accomplish dark deeds. Blood-satisfied demons, powered by the thrill of death, become ravenous, unstoppable beasts that are let loose into the Earth, and their mark leaves trails of evil.

Whoever cries out to God will be saved by the blood of Christ because God only plays by the rules. A sincere cry is all that is needed. Hell is guided by a lack of ethics, but it cannot intercept the blood of Christ or stop its power because Jesus Christ is Lord. The truth is, the evil one does not tamper with the blood of Christ because it would cleanse his sinful soul. In the Book of Hebrews, the writer tells us that after His resurrection, Jesus went into Heaven itself and presented the Father God with the pure sacrifice of His shed blood. He offered His blood as the eternal payment for all who choose to accept God's plan of salvation. The enemy profits from the lives he keeps locked in the spiritual chains of bondage. He owns these lives, but he is a cruel slave master who profits from the disgrace of his slaves. The only way out is the shed blood of Jesus Christ. Through His sacrifice on the cross, Christ earned redemption for man. Every bondage of sin was destroyed at Jesus' crucifixion. As He hung on the cross, His report was, "It is finished; man's redemption is paid."

In the spirit world, each life carries significant value. Each life that is taken and each drop of blood that is spilled weighs monumentally to the owner of that life. When servants of the Devil die, those lives belong to him, and those souls find no rest with their Father God. The enemy profits from lost souls. Those who have humbled and buffeted themselves to avoid the traps of evil, find rest in the loving arms of God when their season on Earth is over. God has reserved beautiful rewards and treasures for those who have conquered the snares and traps set here on Earth.

Before the end, every man is invited into redemption to be restored. The blood of Christ settles all spiritual matters. It pays for sins, it acquits the guilty by laying the sin on another, and it restores spiritual life. All who were unclean are made pure after being washed with the blood of Christ. Then the blood of Christ continues to work until it brings the sanctified one into righteousness.

Please know that as you continue to yield yourselves as servants by obedience; obedience to God leads you unto righteousness. (Romans 6:16).

Righteousness, not goodness. There is a clear difference between goodness and righteousness. Goodness can be attained by concentrated efforts and by choice. Righteousness is not a human characteristic. It is the character of God given as a free gift to those who have chosen Christ and the plan of salvation. Righteousness is the work which the hands are given to do that yields a profit for God. It is like digging diamonds out of a rock; extremely tedious and extremely rewarding. It is called righteousness because it is an impossible task if it is not bestowed by God and fueled by grace. Therefore, it is righteousness and not goodness that places man in a God-centered relationship.

So then, redemption leads to ownership, then to obedience, then to righteousness, then to being born-again.

Jesus answered, *I tell you the truth, no one can enter into and receive the benefits of the kingdom of God unless he is born of water and of the Spirit. Flesh gives birth to flesh, but the Spirit gives birth to spiritual babies. You should not be surprised that God requires you to be born again.* (John 3:5–8).

For those who are born again, the thief cannot steal your soul then dangle it before your eyes so you can chase him down to Hell. When you are born again, the hole that was in your heart is filled, and with gratitude you enjoy life and your relationship with your Father God.

Just being a good person does not activate a change of ownership. Obedience to sin gave the enemy control, making man his servant. Changing the guards requires more than just good deeds. In fact, no one walks out of the dungeon of evil and becomes *good*. First, the stain of evil must be washed away by the blood of Christ. Second, the heart must repent. Repentance is to despise the deeds of the past to the degree that they become repulsive. To become a legitimate servant of God, one who belongs to God must be marked by the blood of Christ. Since man was sold into sin at birth, the change, the escape, requires the blood of Jesus Christ.

Men who choose to dispute the birth of the Lord Jesus Christ, His deity, His sovereignty, and the existence of God, should reconsider. Satan, the enemy of mankind's soul, cannot afford to entertain that notion, or his kingdom would cease to exist. Of course, it is just another sinister lie in his bag of tricks to win another life, but he himself can never indulge. That would be the end of evil here on Earth. Those of us who have lived long enough know the Devil is not stupid.

No man can come to the Father but by Jesus Christ. (John 14:6).

Every man must first be plunged into the cleansing fountain of Christ before entering into the bliss of God the Father. The escape from Hell (salvation) cannot be found in any other source, *for there is no other name under Heaven by which men must be saved.* (Acts 4:12). To accept Jesus Christ as Lord and Savior is to believe in and submit to the legal agreement of the purchase that took place through Christ. Man must trust Jesus Christ to bring about eternal life. Jesus Christ is an offering of purity. No one else has been found pure in the eyes of God to satisfy the offering of the unblemished sacrifice of blood.

Now, the virgin birth makes sense. God, the Creator, needed a sacrificial lamb for mankind. Not a sacrificial animal for man, but the giving of human sacrifice for human redemption. God designed a special creation in the form of His Son. In order not to tamper with the laws of Earth, this spiritual plan had to be offered to and accepted by a human. The Virgin Mary accepted the plan when she said, *Be it unto me according to Your Word.* (Luke 1:38). The Holy Spirit overshadowed her and implanted the Son of the Lord God in her womb. There was no commingling of the mother's and baby's blood or there would have been a breach and the high possibility of termination of the fetus. So, Jesus, the Son of God, was given to the Earth, born of a woman (which made Him human); but the holy seed was knowledgeable in all the wisdom of God. Jesus then accomplished His life's purpose with the ultimate focus and offered His blood for the purchase of man from the evils of the Devil.

We cannot cross over into the prosperity and peace of God without the blood of Christ. Taking the hands-off approach simply says, *I wish to remain a servant to him who owns me.* To have audience with God the Father, we must accept and honor the sacrifice of the shed blood of Jesus Christ. Jesus Christ is the door to our Father God.

6

Blood As a Covering

*To be covered with the blood of Jesus Christ,
is to be protected by the life of Christ.*

Imagine looking at the bloom of an iris and feeling ashamed for the flower because its internal parts are exposed. This was the misfortune Adam and Eve experienced in the Garden of Eden. Sin entered into something that was holy and made it a curse, making it ugly to the point where it had to be covered. The act of sin uncovers and strips man of the Presence and the Glory of God, leaving him spiritually unprotected and in a state of nakedness. After sin is committed, man can feel the curse approaching, and guilt says there is nothing you can do to stop it. The curse leaves man bare, an open target to the assault and torment of the foes from Hell. Sin is a package deal; it brings shame, it brings fear, it brings guilt; and guilt opens her arms to torture. If sin had no guilt, the curse would not be effective. Guilt is mentally accepting the punishment that comes with the package of sin.

The worst part of this sin package deal is that every participant is pulled in through the promise of a lie. If the Devil opened his hand and made a full disclosure of sin, he would have no followers. He must promise pleasure and he must promise to restore all he stole. "You had no one to father you, to care or listen to your concerns. Here, let me offer you someone who cares." All lies. Full disclosure would be, "I stole your father's heart then drove him away from his family. Now, I am offering you the same deal. I am about to destroy your heart and drive you away from your family." Sin promises lies. Everyone who is hooked by the bait becomes cursed, uncovered, and loaded with guilt.

For covering to be restored, there must be atonement. Atonement is payment sufficient to cover the damages of the crime, payment that erases the deeds of the crime, and payment strong enough to restore everything back to order. Atonement is the voice of authority and power within the blood of Christ. The definition of atonement written in the law books of the spirit says, "The blood of Christ has the authority to choose its candidates at will and the power to loose any shackle so that the candidate may enter into peace with God and be made holy.

Seven days you shall make atonement for the altar and sanctify it. Then it shall be an altar most holy, and whatsoever touches the altar shall be holy. (Exodus 29:37).

Sin, which is disobedience to God's Word and His will, is a spiritual act carried out in the Earth, and because it is spiritual, it requires spiritual payment. Blood is the only covering that satisfies the payment for sin. Blood is the currency of the spirit world. Blood covers the ones it purchases, and that indicates ownership. God said, *Whenever I see the blood, I will pass over you.* (Genesis 12:13): indicating that the blood has distinctive qualities identified in the spirit world and provides protection or distinction to whomever it covers.

The blood of Jesus Christ is the perfect spiritual covering. Those who are covered in the blood of Jesus are honored and treated as sacred in the eyes of Almighty God. The principle is the pure for the impure, the clean for the unclean, the whole for the broken: truth restored where deceit was sown. The perfect covering has to be free from sin, and the sacrifice has to be blood. Adam and Eve covered themselves with leaves, but that was a physical attempt to fix the spiritual problem of sin. Leaves could not restore their status or cover their sins. We know this because they hid from God when He came calling, indicating that the guilt and shame of sin were still present.

Sufficient covering is restorative. God properly covered Adam and Eve when He shed the blood of an animal, and in the spirit, they were adequately covered—atoned for. Atonement restores. Animals have no sin, no intellectual nature to render their lives unholy. Man does.

Man sins with understanding, whether deceived or not, presumptuous or drawn by uncontrollable lust—man sins by choice.

God set in place the use of holy blood to cover sins. Interestingly, the Bible does not offer an explanation why this life-giving substance was chosen as a spiritual tool, except that it carries life. As a result, we see that God has distributed Himself in every man through blood. Every man is a carrier: every man is a carrier of the DNA of God. A bit of God is displayed in the Earth through every man. Other intellectually suitable answers can be linked to the physical functions of blood. Where it establishes a state of equilibrium and provides nutrients for the body, we can also see the life of God, breathed into man with the same function. The function of defense and waste removal is equal to the covering and protection God provides through the work of redemptive blood. Finally, all things being equal, the blood of Jesus Christ our Lord places us in a state of spiritual health with our Father God.

The Bible tells us that all life carries the breath of God. At the end, when man dies, he gives up that breath, and the frame goes limp. We know that God formed man from dust, and man, when he dies and is buried, blends once again with dust. In our limited understanding, we have learned to grasp these concepts because we see them every day. Yet God takes life a bit further by telling man that we are created in His image. Image in its proper context would mean form, but in an intended context, it would mean containing the basic functional quality to become the offspring of the Creator Himself. Jesus, in His glorified body, just prior to His ascension, is the picture of man in the image of God. The resurrected Christ was a man in purity, a man who was no longer vulnerable to the enemy of life. This is the man who triumphed over sin and death, a man in unique oneness with His maker in image and in a state of purity.

There is truly a divine connection between God and man. Our Father who lives in Heaven is doing everything in His power to get man to make his way back to his heavenly home. There exists a Love so pure and so sweet that it binds the heart of God to His children. God did not hesitate to offer His Son as the ultimate sacrifice for man. At the hands of man, the Lord of Glory, the Son of God, was shamefully and brutally tortured and strung-up on a cross. Not even that torture could deter the love of God: nothing that man has done can change the love of God for him. But wait, the opposite must also be true. There truly is a Hell and it is ruled by the hater of all flesh, whose sole existence is to cheat man out of the love of Christ.

Satan is viciously planning the defeat of all men. At the end of each day, he goes back to his camp and counts the number of souls he was able to steal. Jesus came to give life and to snatch men out of the path of evil. Jesus Christ sacrificed His blood freely so that man would have a protective shield against the darts of Hell. Jesus offers the only answer for the once-and-for-all covering for the sins of mankind. Those who believe and accept Christ's blood as a covering are free from the bitterness and sting of death.

The sting of death is sin, and the strength of sin is the law. But thanks be to God, who gives us the victory through our Lord Jesus Christ. (Corinthians 15:56–57).

The soul that sins, it shall die. (Ezekiel 18:20).

Sin automatically removes the presence of God, but it cannot remove the love of God. Only man can push God away.

What sacrifice does the enemy make for those who serve him? Satan has nothing to offer those who have dedicated their time to honoring him. For those who have spent their time furthering his kingdom, he inflicts them with the fear and torment of the sting of sin and death. Let the truth be told, he has nothing but evil to offer. Satan is impotent in the spiritual realm; he is truly a has-been. Whatever he claims to offer as a reward is not an offer at all. He pressures man into acting out against God in exchange for a moment of pleasure; that is no offer. He has but a short time to play this game of deceit, and he plays it well. At the end comes the judgment, and his game will end.

The holy blood of Christ is reverenced in the spirit world as the signature of God on man's life. When man receives the blood of Christ as a covering, it silences the pressures of Hell. No more can the darkness of evil just waltz in the front door and order man into surrender. The blood-covered saints are protected from evil.

Yea, though I walk through the valley of the shadow of death, I will fear no evil. (Psalm 23:4).

To cure sin, God set up the plan of an even exchange of life for life. Satan called the shot of sin upon all by deceiving the first man, Adam. Now, Jesus Christ calls the shot of atonement for whosoever believes in Him. Jesus was not of Adam's vein, for Mary conceived the child by the overshadowing of the Holy Spirit. Jesus is free from the label sinner and became the perfect offering, the perfect exchange for a sinful life.

Blood is marked by its purity, both in the natural world and in the spirit. In the spirit world, pure blood is marked as the blood of Christ. Whoever accepts the blood of Christ is covered with the spiritual cloak of divine angelic protection. Covering also means that the power of Christ is deposited in the lives of those who have received the blood. These are the saints who have been born again and hidden in God through Christ.

I am crucified with Christ. I am not alive; it is Christ that is alive in me. The life that I now live in the flesh, I live by the faith of the Son of God, who loves me and gave Himself for me. (Galatians 2:20).

...I am found in Christ, not having my own righteousness, which is of the law. I am living a life of faith, which means, the things I do come from listening to God and being a tool in God's hands. God is working out this righteousness in me, the more I increase in faith. All this working means I am tuned in to Him and I know Him; I experience the power of His resurrection, and I endure sufferings because of Christ. I apply my heart to do all God asks, even unto death. (Philippians 3:9–10).

In Him, the born-again are tucked away under the wings of their Lord, sanctified, and made heirs of the inheritance according to the eternal purpose of God the Father. Those who have been purchased by His blood become God's possession because they believe by faith and partake of His promise! Then all glory and honor to Him who is able to do exceedingly abundantly above all we can ask or think, because His power works in us. All glory be to Him, forever and ever.

7

Blood Speaks

The enemy has made no sacrifice for man.
No one can testify to receiving any good from Lucifer.

So far, we have established that blood is alive, blood redeems, and blood covers; now comes the premise that blood speaks. If all this is true, this tissue is not merely a necessary component of the anatomy. No other tissue, organ, or system alone has earned the credence of blood. Some organs, like the liver, can function on as little as 30 percent capacity; others can be removed without tremendous effects on the body. However, as soon as the blood cell count is lowered, it begins to speak. When the doctor says the cell count is low, there is cause for great concern, and the emphasis is on how to raise them back to normal levels.

Beyond its physical tones, blood has a spiritual voice. Man does not have the ability to hear blood audibly, but switch realms, and blood speaks. In Genesis 4, the sons of Adam and Eve (Abel and Cain) brought their gifts and made a presentation to God. God accepted Abel's offering but not Cain's. The rejection of the gift was so intolerable to Cain that he rose up in anger and killed his brother.

The Lord God visited Cain and asked, "Where is Abel, your brother?"

Cain replied, "Why are You asking me? I do not know where he is. Am I my brother's keeper?"

Then God laid it out: *"The voice of your brother's blood is crying to Me from the ground. You are cursed from the Earth, which has opened her mouth to receive your brother's blood from your hand."* (Genesis 4).

God heard the cry of Abel's blood and responded to the cry by cursing Cain. Cain became a fugitive and a vagabond in the Earth after the curse. His skill was wasted; nothing worked in his favor anymore.

The Earth and its treasures became elusive, like a shadow to the man. He aimlessly occupied space on the Earth until his death.

Bloodshed has become a normal part of man's livelihood. It is natural to hunt or domesticate animals and kill them for food. The purpose of shedding blood makes all the difference.

In Leviticus 17, God laid out the law on this matter. *Whoever kills an ox, or lamb, or goat (in the camp or outside the camp) and does not bring it to the door of the Tabernacle as an offering to the Lord, that the priest may sprinkle the blood upon the altar and burn the fat for a sweet savor unto the Lord, has offered this blood to devils after whom they are lusting for the treasures and bounty of the Earth. That person will be held responsible for the shed blood, and I will cut him off from his people. This will become the law forever and will apply to strangers or anyone that comes among you. Do not offer burnt offerings or sacrifices of blood to devils, or I, the Lord God, will set My face against that soul who eats or sacrifices blood unto devils.*

For the life of the flesh is in the blood, and I have given it to you upon the altar to make an atonement for your souls. For it is the blood that makes an atonement for the soul. (Leviticus 17:11).

David was King of Israel, a man chosen by God for a great task. During his reign, David decided to build a temple for the Lord, but God told King David not to build Him a temple because he had blood on his hands.

God said to me, 'You shall not build a house for My Name, because you have been a man of war and have shed blood.' (1 Chronicles 28:3).

Here is part of the story. King David, taking a stroll on his roof one day, laid eyes on a beautiful woman taking a bath. David ignored sound reasoning and decided to make the woman his. He discovered that she was married, but that did not deter his passion. Instead, he gave orders that the woman's husband be killed so he could freely indulge.

The Bible speaks of this king as a man after God's own heart. Many of the Psalms, or songs of praise, were written by him, and it is obvious that this king sought to live for God. Failure of this magnitude, recorded in the Bible and handed down to us, must carry a noteworthy message. Though David repented, the stench of blood spoke in the nostrils of God. King David had a vision to build a temple in Jerusalem in honor of his God. The plans he laid out for the temple made it a great monument. It seems as if this temple would have marked a significant achievement in the life of this king, but the lot fell to his son. Today, the glory of one of the greatest temples built on Earth is attributed to his son, Solomon.

In the land of Ur of the Chaldeans, God called a man named Abraham and began to speak with him as a man would speak to a friend. God promised Abraham to make from his loins a great nation; a nation exclusive to God, with laws, rituals, a land they would call home, and a special covenant. This covenant between God and His friend was made by blood. God told Abraham to remove the foreskin of every male child born to him, and this would become a blood-ownership covenant between them. God would be their God, and the token of circumcision became the covenant between them forever.

And I will establish My covenant between Me and you and your children after you for generations as an everlasting covenant, to be a God unto you and to your children forever. I will give to you, and to your children after you, the land where you are strangers. I will give you all the land of Canaan for an everlasting possession, and I will be your God. You shall keep My covenant; you, your children, and all their children. This is My covenant:

every male child among you shall be circumcised, and it shall be a token of the covenant between Me and you. (Genesis 17:7–11).

Many years later, the children of Abraham (the Israelites) became slaves to the Egyptians. Four hundred years of bondage is no ordinary matter. Imagine recounting your earthly achievements only to say you lived your entire life as a slave. These people did not give up on the promise of God. In their flesh, they had a covenant with the Most High God, and they never allowed slavery to steal the covenant. In due time, God came to their rescue, and He rescued them by plaguing the spirit of Pharaoh. The first plague against Egypt on behalf of the children of Israel was blood.

The Lord spoke to Moses, Say unto Aaron, 'Take your rod and stretch out your hand over the waters of Egypt, upon their streams, their rivers, their ponds, and upon all their pools of water, that they may become blood. And there will be blood throughout all the land of Egypt, both in vessels of wood and in vessels of stone.' (Exodus 7:19).

This plague came from the ground and is symbolic of the blood of those who died from the cruelty of the hands of Pharaoh. Over four hundred years of blood rising up, crying, bringing a stench, bringing thirst, destroying the food supply, tormenting the minds of the living, wreaking havoc on the land; speaking its language in earthly tones.

The process of deliverance from slavery was carried out in phases. One after another, plagues were poured out on the land of Egypt until God was ready to release the Israelites completely from bondage. The last plague on the land of Egypt was not commanded until atonement through a spotless lamb was made. Every plague that God sent to Egypt tormented the minds of the Egyptians but did not carry the power to free the Israelites from bondage. The moment God was ready, the voice of blood had to make a wailing cry up to Heaven on behalf of the slaves—atonement. The voice of the blood of pure and spotless lambs came into the ears of God.

The people changed their lives by following God's instructions of blood. Before God shows His glory, before He fulfills His promise, before God brings us into our desired haven, before God answers the wailing of the soul, He ordains blood.

And Moses said, "Thus says the Lord, 'About midnight I will go out into the midst of Egypt, and all the firstborn in the land of Egypt shall die. From the firstborn of Pharaoh that sits upon his throne, even unto the firstborn of the maidservant that is behind the mill, and all the firstborn of beasts. And there shall be a great cry throughout all the land of Egypt such as there was none like it, nor shall be like it anymore. But against any of the children of Israel shall not a dog move his tongue, against man or beast. That you may know that the Lord does make a difference between the Egyptians and Israel.'" (Exodus 11:4–7).

Never had God given such a mandate. Blood filled the land in the beginning, and blood filled the land at the end. The currency of the spirit was sufficiently offered and received. The invoice was stamped, *Paid in Full*. That night, God crushed Pharaoh's spirit with a death blow. God crushed the empire by taking the heir, the hope of Egypt, and other possible heirs who were eligible to reign and carry on the inherited legacy. Not only that, but God recompensed Pharaoh for his unthinkable act of killing the male children at the time Moses was born.

Before the Exodus came the Passover: a holy sacrifice of a spotless lamb, chosen and precious, dear to the Father's heart. The Passover was given as a gift of love to a wounded people—a people without strength, a broken people. To rise up from the ashes of defeat, there must be the offering and the receipt of blood—blood that is pure, holy, and free of sin. A holy covenant of blood, made by those in need to a holy God, becomes a holy bondage breaker.

God's instructions were clear. He told Moses to speak to all the congregation of Israel and say to them, *On the tenth day of this month, every man shall take a lamb for each house.* (Exodus 12:3). The lamb chosen was to be without blemish and a male of the first year. It could be taken from the sheep or from the goats, and the people were to keep it until the fourteenth day of the same month. After the fellowship with this chosen lamb, the whole assembly of the congregation of Israel was instructed to kill it in the evening, then take the blood, and strike it on the two side posts and upper doorposts of the houses where they ate the roasted flesh. Further, they were to eat it in haste, with their loins girded, shoes on their feet, and staffs in their hands—a preparation for the Exodus. It was the Lord's Passover.

Then the Lord continued, "For I will pass through the land of Egypt this night and will smite all the firstborn in the land of Egypt, both man and beast. Against all the gods of Egypt, I will execute judgment. I am the Lord." (Exodus 12:12).

The common thread in the language of blood is revenge for the weak, from God, who heard the cry of the slain. We can lift our heads in confidence, knowing that God's ears are not deaf so that He cannot hear, His hands are not shortened so that He cannot save, and He is a defender of the defenseless.

But let's stand in the shoes of the Cains, the King Davids, and the Pharaohs of the world. What circumstances impale themselves upon mankind, leaving man in the throes of darkness so that without compassion for the sanctity of life, he can commit the act of slaying his brother? How does he free himself from the talons and vices of death that both enslave and mockingly cry against him?

Jesus told the crowd, *Come unto Me, all you who labor and are heavy laden, and I will give you rest. Take My yoke upon you and learn of Me, for My yoke is easy and My burden is light.* (Matthew 11:28-30).

Jesus Christ will make a covenant with whomever, if only they seek Him with all their hearts. Isn't it marvelous to know that by choice and subsequent obedience, we are distinguished to enter the Presence of the Lord God Almighty?

8

Spirit, Water, and Blood

Whoever is born of God overcomes the world.
1 John 5:4

Just as blood connects with the spirit world, water is used in spiritual matters, but to a much lesser degree. Water is indispensable throughout the world, in every culture, for recreation, food, health, industry, agriculture, and cleansing. Water is also part of an important religious ritual called *Baptism*; used by the followers of Christ and in other religions.

What is water? More than 70 percent of the Earth is covered in water. More than 60 percent of the body's content is water. Amniotic fluid is water; spinal fluid is water; tears are water; saliva, mucus, and lymph contain water. Forty percent of the cells contain water, but most significantly, 55 percent of blood is water. There is just a sense that water has utmost importance, but its abundance may have caused us to overlook its value.

The inauguration of Jesus' ministry on Earth took place by baptism in the river Jordan. Each gospel writer of the New Testament was also careful to document the baptism of Jesus by water. John the Baptist immersed Jesus in water, and as He came up out of the water, the Spirit of God descended upon Him, then a declaration was heard by those around as God announced, *This is My beloved Son in whom I am well pleased.* (Matthew 3:17).

Jesus fulfilled the spiritual connection between Heaven and Earth. His ministry started with water, after which the Holy Spirit descended upon Him, and He engaged in the blood of Passover. Neither the Bible nor history gives record of Jesus' life between the ages of twelve and the time of His baptism. However, after the initiation in water, the documented life of His ministry began. Water baptism and the descending of the Holy Spirit qualified Him to begin His ministry. The miracles, the teachings, and the power to not be overcome by or sink into the quagmire of the culture, had to wait for the baptisms of water and of the Spirit. Jesus became born again. It was in being born again that God released His authority upon Jesus. Born again meant that the Father signed His approval: that is, full authority from God to do that which He was sent to the Earth to do.

Baptism, as it has been handed down to us, has taken on different meanings to different denominations. However, the Bible tells us in Galatians 3 that as many as are baptized into Christ have put on Christ. It is further clarified in Colossians 2, that baptism is a burial of the past with its sins, and as the believer is raised out of the water, a mysterious work of God will begin. Baptism, then, is a spiritual burial. All of the past is washed away, and a new life in Christ begins. All who have been baptized in Christ are spiritually covered and protected in Him.

The process makes the believer alive in Christ with sins forgiven. The roadblocks that stemmed from past sins which stood against that person, are blotted out. So many of us can speak of recurring patterns of failure in life that do not allow us to go further or to prosper. Baptism cancels the authority of these spirits, disarms them, and causes the believer to begin experiencing victories. Before baptism, the believer had no power to fight nor any understanding to make changes. After being raised up out of the water and being filled with the Spirit of God, life changed by the Spirit of God. No longer do the spirits of darkness have permission to play their games of evil. Permission was removed as the past went under the water. Water broke the bonds and washed away the connection to the spirits that held the lid of oppression.

In St. John 3, the story is told of Nicodemus, a Jewish ruler who came to Jesus, inquiring of His miraculous power. "Jesus, you don't seem to be stopped by the forces that block the rest of us. You perform miracles, You heal diseases, You free people from the demons they lived with for years. You lack nothing, You are always in good spirits—how do You do it?"

Jesus responded, "You must be born again. You must be born of water and of the Spirit. If you understand this, you will never perish. When you are born again, it will open your spiritual understanding because it is just like the wind. Once you have entered into it, you can see and feel the effects of it, but you cannot tell how it happens."

There are three that bear witness in Heaven: the Father, the Word, and the Holy Spirit; and these three are one. There are three that bear witness on Earth: the Spirit, the water, and the blood; and these three agree as one. (1 John 5:7-8).

There is an indispensable relationship on the Earth between Spirit, water, and blood, and the three in unison transmit signals into the spirit world. The signals communicate with God the Father, and through the power of God, they destroy the forces of evil. Water and blood work like a completed electrical circuit that begins to function when plugged into the socket of the Spirit.

Just as it is in the spirit world, so it is in the body. Every tissue of the body is either immersed or suspended in water, then saturated by blood, and controlled by the spirit of man. (Without the spirit, the body is dead.) The body enjoys a state of equilibrium when blood, water, and the spirit of man are in unison.

God invites every man to tap into the mystery of His Holy Spirit and make that intimate connection with Him. When man gets hungry for the Presence of God, the Holy Spirit baptizes the body and the soul, which purifies and cleanses them from sin. This purification and cleansing prepare man to enter into a seamless connection with God.

As man enters into the covenant with God, the Holy Spirit leads him to communion with the blood of Jesus Christ. Baptism in the Holy Spirit, water baptism, covenant with the Father God, and communion with the blood of Christ secure the union where God becomes one with man. Now, the man is ready to begin a walk of wisdom, knowledge, and fellowship with God. To have a relationship with God, man must be born again.

It is the consistent following after the Holy Spirit, the washing of the mind by the word of God, and the communion of the blood of Jesus that make man whole. Giving much attention to the details of life can lead us in directions opposite to the pure nature of God. In this walk of faith, there is a constant need for repentance to maintain an uninterrupted connection with God. Repentance is not a slobbering of tears and confession; instead, it is the conscious conviction that the heart must avoid the traps of darkness. Repentance is a heart posture; it means the heart has turned its attention to God and away from the world. The eyes of the soul are constantly on guard, especially against the things that held it in chains before the power of baptism.

There is no need to feel overwhelmed by the God-natured purity man is required to possess. The nudges of the Holy Spirit to walk in repentance must be seen as love taps. Through the Holy Spirit, God secures His children with the sweetness of cleansing. God speaks sweetly and gently, and as the heart yields to the spoken word, the washing and sanctification cover the heart in love.

Husbands, love your wives, just as Christ loved the Church and gave Himself for it. He sanctified and cleansed it with the washing of water by His Word. Christ went through all this process that He might present to Himself a glorious Church, not having spot, or wrinkle, or any such thing, but that it should be holy and without blemish. (Ephesians 5:25–27).

Continuous cleansing is a must! After we have been baptized by water into the faith of Christ, we continue to wash away the bugs that creep into our lives by being baptized in the word of God.

Many religions require the religious ritual of baptism. For some, it is immersion in water, and for others, it is the sprinkling of water, but the intent is the need for cleansing. Just as baptism in Christ washes man clean of the deeds of past sins or past involvements, so baptism into any other group washes the individual clean of the involvement in any previous religion. Baptism is a washing that sets the individual apart into that specific religion.

It is commonly known that a visit to the voodoo priest or the witch doctor requires washing. For the ritual to be effective, the seeker must be washed clean of any past religious involvement, especially of the power of Christ. The work of the crucified Savior, Jesus Christ, must be washed away for the work of darkness to take its course. The voodoo priest and the witches who practice religion for Lucifer, understand the power of Jesus Christ. The gospel that Jesus Christ brought to the Earth is that the power of God is now available to man so that man will not have to be subjected to works of evil. The power in the gospel of Jesus Christ incinerates every work of evil. No longer do the righteous have to seek help from the voodoo man, or visit with the psychic to get direction for the future, or chant with the witches to gain power. The gospel has arrived. The good news is God is now with us.

When the Roman soldiers were ready to take their victims from the cross at the time of Jesus' crucifixion, a lance was used to pierce Jesus' side. Instantly, blood and water, distinctly separate, flowed from the puncture. Medical evaluations concluded there was a buildup of fluid in the chest cavity due to hemorrhaging from the continuous beatings. The hemorrhaging caused the liquid portion of blood to separate from the cells and other particles in the blood, yielding what has been written as 'blood and water flowing from His side.' Medical laboratories separate the liquid portion of blood from its particles using a centrifuge—a force that spins the blood at high speeds. Trauma to the chest caused the buildup of fluid in the lungs; the fluid became trapped in the air sacs of the lungs, and the constant beatings forced the separation of particles. This sacrifice was designed to become a fountain of healing for those who have been wounded by sin and deprived of love.

Jesus Christ wrote the spiritual page in the Heavens that made it legal for sins to be washed away by the connection of Spirit, water, and blood. The holy Son of Heaven spilled blood and water on the Earth, a divine execution of holiness washing the Earth. Every tear that man sheds because of the pains of darkness connects with the sacrifice of the cross of Christ and unites the heart of God with His children. God lost His children to sin in the garden of Eden, but He redeemed the lost as the blood of His son flowed from the cross. The demanding cry of holy blood has become salvation. Salvation is the answer that is written into law by the Holy Judge concerning the sins of man. The answer is that man is no longer alone in his struggle against evil; now blood is appealing on his behalf. In man's weakness, blood cries. In his loneliness, blood cries. In his depression, blood cries. Where man has been emptied of his abilities and worth and dragged into the dungeon of despair, the holy blood of the Son of God has been spilled and will never keep silent until justice is served on the head of evil.

That is the reason Jesus said, "You must be born again." Born again is not the impossibility of living up to the holiness of God. Born again is man yielding himself to God through the blood of Jesus Christ so that the blood, the water, and the Holy Spirit may cry out against the darkness that hides, waiting to trap his soul. Born again means agreeing with Christ so that the unity of Christ and man may result in a covenant with God. It means the yielding of the body to Christ, the entrusting of the mind to the Holy Spirit, and the constant washing of water by the word, becoming the joy of man. This covenant of agreement with God, of man uniting with God, allows God's glory to satisfy every longing desire of man.

John, in his revelation, caught a glimpse of Christ as the Word of God. Christ is not a judge, and Christianity is not a set of strict rules set up to make life difficult for the follower. Christ is the door to our Holy God. As man honors the words of Christ, he becomes like Christ; he becomes one with Christ. There is no struggle when he honors the word, because the word changes the man, even his heart. Those who are immersed in the Word, in the truth of God, are those who are plugged into divine unity with God.

Baptism buries the old man, and the man that rises out of the water is quickened, a new spiritual man, able to attain the realms of the Spirit. Quickening means bonded together with Christ. Jesus and His disciples were immersed in water baptism, which explains the mysterious agreement that united them as one.

Jesus paved the way for man through the shedding of His blood: He triumphed over the principalities and powers of Hell. Those who say *Yes* to being baptized in Christ are pulled into the spiritual authority of Christ and are seated in heavenly places in Christ. None of this makes sense until *Yes* becomes true surrender. At that point, man is no longer in the driver's seat. The Holy Spirit takes over, and man is empowered to rule over the forces of darkness by the Spirit of God, who testifies to the new birth in those who have been purified through baptism.

Just prior to the revelation of the agreement of Spirit, water, and blood on Earth, John made an exciting declaration. "He who overcomes the world, the system, and the clauses set out to trap the heart of man is he who believes and therefore lives by the footprints of Jesus, the Son of God." It is amazing that the truth and glory of God are at our fingertips with complete access found in the simplicity of obedience.

9

God Speaks on the Abominations of Blood

Do not bring an abomination into your house, or you will be doomed to destruction. You must utterly detest it and utterly abhor it, for it is an accursed thing. Deuteronomy 7:26

The Old Testament prophet Ezekiel lived around the time of 622-600 BC. He was from the land of Judah but was taken captive and exiled to Babylon during the first raid of King Nebuchadnezzar. His prophetic words were spoken to the house of Israel, the false prophets, the elders, the priests, and the leaders of the Hebrew nation. The people had strayed from the principles of God. His prophetic words clearly define the requirements of God for His people.

Again, the Word of the Lord came unto me, saying, "Son of man, cause Jerusalem to know her abominations. On the day you were born, your navel was not cut, nor were you washed in water to supple you. You were not salted at all, nor swaddled. No eye pitied you to do any of these unto you, to have compassion upon you. Instead, you were cast out in the open field, to the loathing of your person, on the day you were born. When I passed by you and saw you polluted in your own blood, I said unto you when you were in your blood, 'Live.' Yes, I said unto you when you were in your blood, 'Live.'"

'I caused you to multiply as the bud of the field, and you increased and became great. Now, when I passed by you, it was the time of love. I spread my skirt over you and covered your nakedness. Then I swore to you and entered into a covenant with you, and you became Mine," says the Lord God. "Then I washed you with water. I thoroughly washed away the blood from you, and I anointed you with oil. I also clothed you with embroidered work, girded you with fine linen, and covered you with silk. I decked you with ornaments and put bracelets on your hands and a chain around your neck. I put a jewel on your forehead, earrings in your ears, and a beautiful crown upon your head." (Ezekiel 16:1–6).

To identify the state of the house at the time of this prophecy, the people of Samaria were given the name Aholah, which translates, *her tent or idolatrous sanctuary*, while the people of Jerusalem were given the symbolic name Aholibah, which means, *my tent*. We could add our own interpretation to these names. Her tent and my tent could possibly mean the establishment of her laws or my laws instead of God's law. Further in the Book of Ezekiel, the people were called rebellious and stiff-hearted transgressors. The message Ezekiel brought was a warning to save the people from the horror of a pending doom, the consequence of establishing their own laws, which resulted in abominations to God.

So great was the defilement of God's people that God equated it to the pollution of baking food with human dung. Imagine the stench. Imagine the horror of sitting down to that meal. Such were the requirements of the prophet Ezekiel to communicate the warning. He had to make God's people understand the holiness of God. God told Ezekiel to do gross things so that human reasoning would have an idea of the extent to which they had nauseated the Holy One and the fierceness of the wrath about to be poured out.

It would not be redundant to repeat that this message was for the people of God, the called, the chosen, the priests, and the leaders of the Church. These were the people called by His Name. To be called by His Name means man adds a surname to his given name. Instead of only Tom Peterson, it becomes Tom Peterson God's Son. Peterson means, the son of Peter, heir to the estate of Peter, and an expectation to live by the standards of the sons of Peter. To be called by the name of our Father God establishes that our connection with God is not superficial but a legitimate claim of belonging. Ezekiel brought a reminder to the nation that it was sacrilegious to know God yet limit their involvement to convenience.

God was against the altars, and images, and idols of the high places where the nation worshiped evil gods. Altars were built in elevated regions, like hills or mountains, and blood sacrifices were made on these altars to various gods.

I am broken with your whorish heart, which has departed from Me, and with your eyes, which go a-whoring after idols. You shall hate yourselves for the evils and abominations that you have committed. (Ezekiel 6:9).

The land had become full of bloody crimes and the city full of violence because of the nation's abominations. Destruction came, and the people searched for peace and found none. The Word of God perished from the priest, and wise counsel was not found in the elders.

In Chapter 8, Ezekiel was shown abominable drawings or symbols on the wall of the court with women weeping after a strange god, and in the Lord's house, men sat worshiping the sun while turning their backs on God. Again, the very next verse shows that the land was filled with violence because of these abominations.

Violence in the land stems from man's lack of reverence towards God. The pattern is disregarding God first, followed by contempt for each other. When man is brazen enough to talk against God and turn his back on God, the outcome will surely be disastrous. No one can blatantly disrespect the holiness of the Lord God Almighty yet find it in their hearts to respect and love each other. Violence comes naturally when moral guidelines are fuzzy. If there is no reverential fear or sense of awe for the holiness and sovereignty of the Almighty God and His Word, who or what can restrain man from the spirit of evil—the insanity that comes to push him over the edge?

It is sobering to hear God continually refer to His people as His own special people. The startling contrast between the abomination and the holiness of God would make it necessary for God to cast off and be done with the evil abominators. But rejection is an evil trait, and God has no part in evil. The warning is not a threat to destroy His beloved but a tug of conviction on the heart to turn from the paths of destruction. God is entreating His children to choose holiness, as He would be powerless to prevent the curse that naturally results from the sin of abomination.

And your elder sister Samaria, and your younger sister Sodom, and her daughters, as if it were a very little thing in your eyes, you were more corrupted than them in all your ways. (Ezekiel 16:46–47).

How much more corruption was added to the sin that brought doomed destruction and curses? Adding to the abomination were children who cursed or belittled their parents: natives who oppressed strangers and ill-treated the fatherless and widows; people who despised the things of God and showed no respect for the Sabbath; men who devised lies to commit murder; and those who uncovered their father's nakedness and humbled women who were ceremonially unclean.

"And one has committed abomination with his neighbor's wife, and another has lewdly defiled his daughter-in-law, and another has humbled his sister, his father's daughter. You have taken gifts to shed blood, you have taken bribes and increased, and you have greedily gained from your neighbors by extortion. You have forgotten Me," says the Lord God. "Therefore, I beat my fists at the dishonest profit you have made and at the bloodshed that has been in your midst. Can your heart endure, or can your heart remain strong in the days when I shall deal with you? I, the Lord, have spoken, and I will do it." (Ezekiel 22:11–14).

They have committed adultery, and blood is in their hands, and with their idols have they committed adultery, and have also caused their sons, whom they bore unto me, to pass through the fire. Moreover, this they have done unto Me: they have defiled My sanctuary on the same day and have profaned My Sabbaths. For when they had slain their children to their idols, then they came the same day into My sanctuary to profane it. Lo, this have they done in the midst of My house. And the righteous men, they shall judge them after the manner of adulteresses and after the manner of women that shed blood, because they are adulteresses, and blood is in their hands. (Ezekiel 23:37–45).

All these abominations plunged the city of Jerusalem into captivity. The king of Babylon came with chariots and weapons, tore down the wall that protected the city, then ravished and destroyed everything he could find. He took the best citizens, tied them together like a chain gang, and made them walk approximately 500 miles to Babylon. When they arrived in Babylon, they were sentenced to forced labor and heavy taxes.

Let us walk back in time. The ancestors of the children of Israel lived as slaves in Egypt under the whip of oppression. As slaves, they were owned by the pharaoh of Egypt. It had to be the hand of God that caused Pharaoh to allow over half a million Jews to pack up and leave town. God saw the cruelty which they endured and gave them specific instructions on how to be released from this impossible bondage. And it worked. So dutifully, very dutifully, every year, Israel observed the instructions of God called the *Passover*. The observance was a reminder of the power of freedom, but also to prevent the possibility of any future oppression and enslavement. Considering the diligence of Israel in observing the Passover, how was it even possible that they ended up in captivity—again?

The blood of the Passover was a God-given ritual that was proven never to fail. Why didn't the observance of the Passover prevent the captivity of these God-chosen people? What message did the nation lift to God despite their diligent obedience to that which activated, in times past, such a mighty deliverance? There is a sense that these questions contradict and yet answer themselves.

Conscientious commitment to a ritual causes it to lose its effectiveness in matters of holiness and godliness when man's heart is drawn away from God. It is commitment to God that connects the heart to the divinity of God, not dutiful obligation to a ritual. The bloodshed and whoredom Ezekiel mentioned clearly violated the laws of holiness. Therefore, participation in the Passover must have been a commingled pollution rather than a celebration of the greatness of God's work. The question can be compellingly answered. Abominations nullify the work of holy blood.

Literally, harlotry violates the principles of blood, as stated clearly in the prophecy of Ezekiel. Mortals are twisted out of shape and take on spirits of jealousy, suicide, hate, murder, and such when betrayed by fornication and adultery. The pungency of the sin creates a despicable taste against the violator, and it does not take a stretch of the imagination for enemies to be born and nurtured for life. Harlotry is grounds for divorce, both in the eyes of God and of man. In the eyes of a holy God, betrayal by the sin of exchanging intimacy for gain is multiplied by even greater powers. God sent warning after warning to the land that had departed from its God.

The challenge God offered through Ezekiel's message was not to a class or sect of the nation or to certain communities so that those in elite standing or of higher stature could frown at the lower-class abominators. The entire nation had come under the guile of the fumes of these abominations. Those who had not strayed into whoredom were not exempt from the violence that reared its ugly head; the darkness was all around. There is nothing symbolic about the darkness of evil. God's priests, prophets, and Church leaders are commanded to be watchmen for those who are vulnerable to sin. Sinners are locked into bondage, and only by a miracle can sinners become free. The Church is saddled with the responsibility of prayer and love so that *men may lead a quiet and peaceable life.* (1 Timothy 2:2).

If leaders fail, followers are doomed. The plan of Hell is to undermine leadership by having them walk the plank of failure. When the bread of failure is baked and served up to a leader, the sweet aroma becomes the blinders that are wrapped securely over the eyes of the followers. Many leaders blindly follow the scent of the dough, defending a rigid point of view, not realizing the trap that lies ahead. The greatest demise of failure is not destruction or the extinction of the structure, but the conversion of the overthrown to serve the conqueror. Whether it is religious, political, financial, or educational, it does not matter what system of leadership is established; sin will destroy it. The opposite is also true: accountability to God and to man, along with adherence to pure values, result in true success.

"If the wicked will turn from all his sins that he has committed and keep all My statutes and do that which is lawful and right, he shall surely live; he shall not die. For I have no pleasure in the death of him that dies," says the Lord God. "Wherefore, turn yourselves, and live." (Ezekiel 18:21, 32).

In his final chapters, Ezekiel's vision was of the restoration of the temple to its rightful state of holiness, with healing waters flowing into the streets. The message is clear: it is with the gathering of the holy saints that God commands His blessings. Therefore, the Church is called to lead the path to holiness. How beautiful that God will take the ugliest, nastiest, most despicable sinner and transform that life into glory and virtue. In fact, no one can claim any goodness; all of us were changed from the filth of sin by His glorious grace.

10

Violations of Blood

*When wisdom enters your heart, and knowledge is pleasant to your soul,
discretion shall preserve you,
and understanding shall keep you. Proverbs 2:10-11*

BLOOD, THE CURRENCY OF THE SPIRIT WORLD ~ 75

The use of blood can stimulate the gates of the spirit and initiate earthly responses. As an important spiritual tool, the misuse of blood will trigger haunting repercussions, and though they often escape our awareness, it does not change the bed of needles on which the violators rest. Let's ponder desecrated uses of blood and their corresponding earthly repercussions.

Blood for Food: The Lord God uncompromisingly forbids the eating of blood for food.

Whatever man of the children of Israel, or of the strangers who dwell among you, who hunts and catches any animal or bird that may be eaten, he shall pour out its blood and cover it with dust; for it is the life of all flesh. Its blood sustains its life. Therefore, I said to the children of Israel, You shall not eat the blood of any flesh, for the life of all flesh is its blood. Whoever eats it shall be cut off. (Leviticus 17:13–15).

Blood of a Virgin: There is something pure and delicate about the eyes of the soul of a virtuous girl. Please note that this is not the girl who has compromised her virtuous standards yet retained parts of her body untouched. Just as a virgin's body is undefiled, so is her mind, and it becomes hard for her to fathom the wiles of the dark spirits that would betray her trust. In the purest sense, she is truly vulnerable and must be protected. Her mind is naïve, and there is almost a sense of trust that the violator would not desecrate her. Dishonoring a virtuous girl is equal to wreaking havoc on every child that her womb produces. The beauty, dignity, and royalty of entering a joyous marital relationship and producing children are robbed when virtue is stolen. As a result, what she produces in marriage is flawed, needing reassurance that goes beyond the capacity of earthly consolers.

If any man takes a wife and goes in to her and detests her and charges her with shameful conduct and brings a bad name on her and says, "I took this woman, and when I came to her, I found she was not a virgin." The father and mother of the young woman shall take and bring out the evidence of the young woman's virginity to the elders of the city at the gate. And the young woman's father shall say to the elders, "I gave my daughter to this man as wife and he detests her. Now he has charged her with shameful conduct, saying, 'I found your daughter not a virgin,' and yet these are the evidence of my daughter's virginity." And they shall spread the cloth before the elders of the city. Then the elders of that city shall take that man and punish him. They shall fine him one hundred shekels of silver and give them to the father of the young woman, because he has brought a bad name on a virgin of Israel. And she shall be his wife; he cannot divorce her all his days. But if the thing is true and evidence of virginity is not found for the young woman, then they shall bring the young woman to the door of her father's house, and the men of her city shall stone her to death with stones, because she has done a disgraceful thing in Israel to play the harlot in her father's house. So, you shall put away the evil from among you. (Deuteronomy 22:13–21).

Blood of Incest: The laws that families could not intermarry were changed by God long after the Earth was established. Noah's daughters were incestuous with their father, and while the story shows that they tricked the poor old man, there were no laws that clearly stated it was wrong. Abraham married his sister, Sarah, and in his culture, it was perfectly normal. While the Children of Israel were in the wilderness, after their encounter with God on the mountain of Sinai, God gave clear instructions that intermarrying between families was to be outlawed.

None of you shall approach anyone who is near of kin to uncover his nakedness; I am the Lord. The nakedness of your father or the nakedness of your mother you shall not uncover. She is your mother; you shall not uncover her nakedness. The nakedness of your father's wife you shall not uncover; it is your father's nakedness. The nakedness of your sister, the daughter of your father, or the daughter of your mother, whether born at home or elsewhere, their nakedness you shall not uncover. The nakedness of your son's daughter or your daughter's daughter, their nakedness you shall not uncover, for theirs is your own nakedness. The nakedness of your father's wife's daughter, begotten by your father—she is your sister—you shall not uncover her nakedness. You shall not uncover the nakedness of your father's sister; she is near of kin to your father. You shall not uncover the nakedness of your mother's sister, for she is near of kin to your mother. You shall not uncover the nakedness of your father's brother. You shall not approach his wife; she is your aunt. You shall not uncover the nakedness of your daughter-in-law; she is your son's wife; you shall not uncover her nakedness. You shall not uncover the nakedness of your brother's wife; it is your brother's nakedness. You shall not uncover the nakedness of a woman and her daughter, nor shall you take her son's daughter or her daughter's daughter to uncover her nakedness. They are near of kin to her; it is wickedness. Nor shall you take a woman as a rival to her sister to uncover her nakedness while the other is alive. (Leviticus 18:6–18).

Female Monthly Cycle: During this time of a woman's life, her body and her emotions are extremely sensitive. Because her reproductive organs are tender and sensitive to touch, God demands that the woman be protected and not violated during this delicate phase. In the Book of Leviticus, God hands down a list of *shall nots;* laws of the forbidden.

You shall not approach a woman to uncover her nakedness if she is in her customary impurity. Moreover, you shall not lie carnally with your neighbor's wife to defile yourself with her. And you shall not let any of your descendants pass through the fire to Molech, nor shall you profane the Name of your God: I am the Lord. You shall not lie with a male as with a woman; it is an abomination. Nor shall you mate with any animal to defile yourself with it. Nor shall any woman stand before an animal to mate with it. It is perversion. (Leviticus 18:19–23).

Blood of Abortion: I wish there was an honest survey of the residual pain and devastation that lives beyond the abortion table. Proportionately, the horror of abortion is relatively 10 percent for the unborn and 90 percent for the parties involved in the taking and sacrificing of the life. The woman who is tricked into the lie of choosing to abort is never told that she will never be able to separate herself from the ghosts of failure. It begins with nightmares, feelings of abandonment, and rejection—even from those who assisted her in the act, and for most women there is the real possibility that the process damages her internal organs. Life after abortion only gets lower and lower. Women who go on to succeed in careers or relationships carry a chip on their shoulder and become bitter, ugly, and nasty for no apparent reason.

The mother is left with haunting feelings, regrets, and an endless search for the love she thought she had found. It is hard to move forward because she attracts the attention of unwholesome and perverted individuals. It seems she is invisible and undesirable to the purity of sound, healthy, lasting relationships. The children she chooses to carry after the ordeal of abortion become victims of the death that lurks inside her womb. The spirit of abortion and death attaches itself to the souls who are born thereafter, leaving victims who become prone to accidents, tragedies, and weird kinds of failures. She walks alone with this tragedy living in her subconscious because no one can truly understand it; therefore, no one can help make it better. As a result, anger takes a seat at her door, betrayal rides her skirt, and a sense of *I deserve this,* leaves her taunted by life's mishaps. The painful secrets of her heart are the many years of unfortunate events that took place before the abortion, over which she felt she had no control. The abortion was only an attempt to make life better. Instead, her choice was a bitter joke.

For it was You who created my inward parts; You knitted me together in my mother's womb. I will praise You because I have been remarkably and wonderfully made. Your works are wonderful, and I know this very well. My bones were not hidden from You when I was made in secret, when I was formed in the depths of the Earth. Your eyes saw me when I was formless; all my days were written in Your book and planned before a single one of them began. (Psalm 139:13–16, HCSB).

Blood of Murder: The loss of a life to the violence of murder ranks highly with any of the greatest pains mankind endures. Loved ones who live with the loss continue life with an emptiness of the soul and an inconsolable sob that can be triggered by even a sound.

It came to pass that Cain brought an offering of the fruit of the ground to the Lord. Abel also brought the firstborn of his flock and their fat. And the Lord respected Abel and his offering, but He did not respect Cain and his offering. And Cain was very angry, and his countenance fell.

So, the Lord said to Cain, "Why are you angry, and why has your countenance fallen? If you do well, will you not be accepted? And if you do not do well, sin lies at the door, and its desire is for you, but you must rule over it."

Now Cain talked with Abel, his brother, and it came to pass, when they were in the field, that Cain rose up against Abel, his brother, and killed him.

Then the Lord said to Cain, "Where is Abel, your brother?"

He said, "I do not know. Am I my brother's keeper?"

And God said, "What have you done? The voice of your brother's blood cries out to Me from the ground. So, now, you are cursed from the Earth, which has opened its mouth to receive your brother's blood from your hand. When you till the ground, it shall no longer yield its strength to you. A fugitive and a vagabond you shall be on the earth." (Genesis 4:3–12).

Blood of Tribal Rituals: Rituals are based on the belief of satisfying a god of some sort and then tapping into the god's power for answers to life's uncertainty. This perception must not be trivialized, because if one cannot attain the power of truth—or more appropriately, the power of God—then settling for lesser powers seems to be a necessary solution. Man knows how to search for power from God's rival, who answers by sacrificial blood. The quest leaves much to be desired, as it does not answer the well-being of the soul or the abundance of life. It merely responds to and satisfies the request for which the blood was shed, leaving the seeker subject to returning again and again, more like a victim of the ritual than a satisfied customer.

The Lord spoke to Moses, saying, "Speak to Aaron, to his sons, and to all the children of Israel, and say to them, 'This is the thing which the Lord has commanded. Whatever man of the house of Israel kills an ox or lamb or goat in the camp, or kills it outside the camp, and does not bring it to the door of the Tabernacle of Meeting to offer an offering to the Lord before the tabernacle of the Lord, the guilt of bloodshed shall be imputed to that man. He has shed blood, and that man shall be cut off from among his people, to the end that the children of Israel may bring their sacrifices, which they offer in the open field, that they may bring them to the Lord at the door of the Tabernacle of Meeting, to the priest, and offer them as peace offerings to the Lord. And the priest shall sprinkle the blood on the altar of the Lord at the door of the Tabernacle of Meeting and burn the fat for a sweet aroma to the Lord. They shall no longer offer their sacrifices to demons, after whom they have played the harlot. This shall be a statute forever for them throughout their generations."(Leviticus 17:1–7).

Blood for Halloween: Halloween is one of the best-kept secrets of a well-told lie. It has penetrated the world by painting a canvas of costumes, candies, and the harmless innocence of ghosts, witches, skeletons, coffins, graves, and scary scenes. Such a misnomer. How can the remains of death that humans revisit yearly in the ghastliest of settings be harmlessly innocent? Those of us whose loved ones have passed on understand the painful emptiness death brings and feel the need to guard our hearts against sorrow. How then can we revisit the frightful portrayal of lives passed on and find it entertaining? So many children have been scarred by the nightmares of Halloween and are afraid to share with their parents the horrors they experience in the night after being exposed to the scary movies and scenes of Halloween.

Research of the meaning of Halloween and its history tells of a day to honor dead saints and to protect the Celts from the dead of the past. History handed down may not be as accurate as it should be, but we have a responsibility to engage in profitable and noble celebrations. Can we enjoy the dead by raising their skeletons and coffins to decorate our yards, then add the gloom of cobwebs, witches, and lights while little kids roam our streets begging for candy; and in the meantime, being ever careful of possible abduction? Shall we also turn a blind eye to the many animals and pets that go missing at Halloween?

He who sacrifices to any god except to the Lord only, he shall be utterly destroyed. (Exodus 22:20).

Defilement through blood speaks a language that is not easily analyzed. It adds a crippling effect to life, and its paralytic symptoms have no rhyme or reason. There is a pattern that creeps up in the lives of those who have tampered with blood. After man has violated blood's sacredness, misfortune sticks like glue. Satan serves up a bowl of soup filled with lies and death and feeds it to unsuspecting souls. As early as the days of Noah, all these abominations existed and were practiced by man. This is proof that man needs God's help to escape the plot of evil laid down before him.

No man (except Christ) has ever walked through life without being trapped by sin, or abominations, or evil. To untangle himself from the trap, he first needs to know that God is not the enemy. God is the strong, loving arm on which he can hold to pull himself out of the dungeon of abomination. What is the strong, loving arm of God? It is forgiveness. Not only does God forgive man, but God also completely wipes away the guilt and shame that comes with abominations and allows man to enjoy the purity of His Presence. When God comes with His love to decorate the lives of those who will let Him in, those who surrender to Him wash their hearts with tears of repentance and God's forgiveness.

11

Jesus' Blood

O Lamb of God, sweet Lamb of God!

As Jesus sat down to the Passover meal with His disciples, He discussed the new testament He was about to establish. This covenant meal may have been roasted lamb, bread without leaven, herbs, and wine. The lamb was slaughtered at the temple, and its blood was given as a sacrifice to the living God. Jesus knew He was sent to the Earth to change the way spiritual business was done. He understood that man is given life to create not just earthly footprints, which fade with time, but spiritual monuments, which are eternal. He had spent the past three years building up a spiritual temple, and this night at the Passover meal, He would put the final bricks in place to complete the new temple of God.

In a matter of hours, Jesus would become the blood sacrifice that would replace the killing of animals during Passover. Every man, at some point in his life, is forced to make a decision about God. At that moment, he will either join a religious group or create one. The decision is based on the sum of all that he knows. Jesus knew His purpose. He knew that He was born to recreate and perfect the Church that Moses started in the wilderness. He would write a new testament, a new covenant that would become the truth that leads men straight to the heart of His Father God. This was His final Passover meal on the Earth because the time for the blood sacrifice of His purpose had come.

Many religious rituals rely on the use of blood to communicate the message of dependence beyond human ability. However, there is a weakness in the method, and that weakness distorts communication. Can the blood of innocent animals who are not able to give consent be used to pardon sins or be used as a true sacrifice? The perfect sacrifice must give consent. The perfect sacrifice must be holy. The ultimate sacrifice must be greater than the sins and the failures of those who need spiritual help. If the sacrifice is not greater, the ritual is inadequate, which means the one to whom the sacrifice is given will always require more and more sacrifices. Blood sacrifices that do not measure up to spiritual requirements lack the power to effect eternal change. Jesus Christ willingly yielded himself to the death of crucifixion, knowing that the shedding of His blood would become the only true currency of the spirit world.

With Jesus' crucifixion pending, a new ritual of the covenant by blood was soon to be instituted. Jesus would die as the sacrificial lamb and change the ritual of the bloodshed of animals used in the Jewish Passover for those who would accept His sacrifice. The difference between Jesus' sacrifice and the sacrifice of animals is that His sacrifice would become a permanent stain on the life of the believer. Instead of having to die again and again, His blood would become the voice of forgiveness in the ear of His Father God.

The Bible tells the story of Judas, a disciple of Jesus, who covenanted with the leaders of the synagogue for thirty pieces of silver in exchange for the capture of Jesus.

Then one of the twelve, called Judas Iscariot, went to the chief priests and said, "What are you willing to give me if I deliver Him to you?" And they counted out to him thirty pieces of silver. So, from that time on, he sought opportunity to betray Jesus. (Matthew 26:14–16).

Later that night, Judas led Roman soldiers to the garden of Gethsemane to arrest Jesus and bring Him face-to-face with the council of priests and Church leaders who were intolerant of His doctrine. To convert the people with His radical beliefs and spout teachings that broke the traditions laid down by Moses was a crime worthy of death under Jewish law. For example, Jesus constantly worked on the Sabbath. He and His disciples, when going on their mission on the Sabbath, with no preparations for the holy day, got hungry and broke corn from the fields. An impotent man at the sheep market pool,

Bethesda, was cured on the Sabbath. To add to the offense, Jesus told the man to take up his bed and walk. The man was not supposed to carry his bed on the Sabbath.

The grievance was that Jesus attracted a large following. Influence of that magnitude would change the statutes of the God of Abraham, Isaac, and Jacob forever. It became absolutely necessary that the clergy of the synagogue take a stand and cure the Nation of this professed Messiah before the wrath of God descended on them all. By priestly standards, the plot to crucify Jesus was justified under the terms of Jewish law.

And the High Priest answered and said to Him, "I put You under oath by the Living God; tell us if You are the Christ, the Son of God!"

Jesus said to him, "It is as you say. Nevertheless, I say to you, hereafter you will see the Son of Man sitting at the right hand of the Power and coming on the clouds of Heaven."

Then the High Priest tore his clothes, saying, "He has spoken blasphemy! What further need do we have for witnesses? Look, now you have heard His blasphemy! What do you think?"

They answered and said, "He is deserving of death."

Then they spat in His face and beat Him; and others struck Him with the palms of their hands, saying, "Prophesy to us, Christ! Who struck You?" (Matthew 26:63–68).

Digging through a bit of history around Jesus' time, the Jewish nation had survived quite a bit of trouble and turmoil after being governed by the Ptolemies and Seleucids. At that time in history, kings would conquer cities and lands, then subject the people to hard labor and cruelty. The Jews were known for their steadfast religious beliefs. To break the spirit of the people, the kings who conquered Jerusalem and Israel would mock their religious rituals. One king sacrificed a pig on the Jewish altar to show his utter disrespect for their religious laws. Josephus, the historian, tells how Pilate used sacred temple money, or Corban, to build a canal to channel water into Jerusalem. It was sacrilegious for the government to use temple money. When protesters gathered, Pilate sent his soldiers dressed as civilians into the crowd. On his signal, the soldiers began to beat and kill the protesters.

These abominations broke the will and the spirit of the people. The stage had been set for a people who were capable of governing themselves, living under the harsh and sacrilegious dictates of outsiders, to round up a mob and declare war before you could flip a coin. The nation was in a state of constant rebellion to protect their God-given traditions and religious rites. Now, to have a Jew, one from within, rise up against their religious beliefs and break the sanctified laws while attracting an enormous following, was treason and worthy of death. The High Priest, Caiaphas, and his council, began mapping the ultimate strategy to make an example of this Jesus. He claimed to be Christ, the Messiah, yet He did not take on the oppressive government that kept the Nation exploited. Caiaphas and his priests began rounding up a mob to create the riot that called for the death of this man, Jesus. Insurrection to advocate for His death was the only solution.

During this time in history, the Jews were under Roman rule and did not have the authority to pronounce the death sentence. Official orders had to come from the governor of Judea, Pontius Pilate, or Herod Antipas, who ruled over Galilee. These governors answered to Julius Caesar, who was over the entire Roman Empire. If Pilate could successfully govern Judea, he would have favor in Caesar's eyes. No small task, as the Jews seemed incapable of giving up their sacred standards for dictators like Pilate. As a ruler, Pilate wanted to leave his stamp on the nation. He was a glamorous ruler. He built life-sized sculptures of himself and made laws based on the standards and ways of the Greeks, which opposed the ways of God. To enforce these desecrated laws, some of the Jews were bribed, but all in all, the nation stood for its principles. These events were tuned and timed precisely into the life of Jesus the Messiah.

Jesus Christ, in the hands of the priests, was the perfect picture of a radical dictator who was finally defeated. To spare cruelty would be equal to sending a signal that another intended Messiah could rise up to lead the nation astray. Nothing was spared to make an example of this man, Jesus, whose given name was Yeshua ben Yosef.

The Sanhedrin (governing council of Jewish priests and leaders) led Yeshua ben Yosef to Pilate's court to ask for his death by crucifixion. There was no small stir among the people, because it was necessary for Pilate to see this matter as a possible riot in the making. With a mob at his doorstep, it would be easier for Pilate to put out the fire by granting Caiaphas and his leaders their wish. If the wish were not granted and a riot ensued, Pilate would again have to report on his ability to govern. Since this was not a matter of State, but one among the people, it was not hard to consent to their wishes and be done with the mob. Not so easy, for Pilate's wife, apparently a woman he trusted, sent a message to him of a troubling dream she had. She said she had suffered many things in the dream, and Pilate should have nothing to do with the just man the Jews wanted crucified.

"I find no fault in this man," Pilate said.

"He teaches heresy against our sacred laws throughout our land, from Galilee to this place." The response was fierce.

Relief came over Pilate at the name Galilee. "Is He a Galilean?" Pilate asked. This was the answer for which he waited. "This man cannot be tried by this court; He belongs under Herod's jurisdiction. Take Him to Herod for your trial."

Patience has a way of solving even the most bewildering trials. The mob and its religious leaders led Jesus away determined under any circumstance to get the death penalty for this danger to the sacred religion of God handed down by their great leader, Moses. It was the day before Passover, and this business had better not drag on, as it would become a pollution of the holy feast. Plus, tending to a prisoner, who would have the time? They had to bring this madness to an end. A verdict was needed immediately, and they would raise hell if it was not granted.

Herod seemed strangely accommodating, more of a welcome to the party than a preparation for trial. As the crowd settled for the trial, Herod faced the man who stirred His Nation with miracles, even raising the dead. Perhaps this man would perform a supernatural wonder for him, and the gods would appear right in his very presence. This trial was history in the making. The chief priests and the scribes presented a rather decisive case. Really, all they wanted was death by crucifixion, and that was clear. Now it was this man's turn to perform his great miracles and make the gods appear.

Herod began with his questions for Yeshua; there was no response. Patience, patience; these spiritual sorts have a framework that requires patience. On and on went the unanswered questions, and Herod grew weary. It did not take long for Herod to realize he was being mocked by this prisoner, who absolutely refused to give him even a flicker of response—mockery of his authority and seat of honor! Quickly, the questions changed their tone, and ridicule and scorn began to pour out on this witty man. But how was he going to defend himself? Surely, he needed to; this crowd would have him dead by nightfall.

"This King of the Jews is not dressed appropriately. Please, bring out a gorgeous robe and array this man like a true king!"

At Herod's command, Yeshua was donned in the finest garb, while the soldiers helped to accommodate the sarcasm of honoring the King of the Jews. To protect his honor, Herod issued mockery as his verdict, and the council was instructed to take him back to Pilate if they wanted him crucified.

Pilate had hoped he had seen the last of this throng. What a stubborn people. Their belief in their God and their steadfast obedience to protect His laws took them beyond human comprehension. Torn between truth and politics, Pilate pulled yet another of his tricks on the disquieted mob.

"I have other prisoners who have desecrated your laws. According to your custom, at the time of your Passover, a prisoner may be released. All these prisoners have been found guilty under your law. I will choose to release this Yeshua ben Yosef and pardon His crimes."

The council of elders and priests would have no such plea. They incited the mob to fury to get the death penalty for Yeshua.

Pilate asked, "What evil has He done?"

The heated crowd would not be swayed. Crucifixion for Yeshua was the only note they chanted. Pilate called for water. He stood before the people, looked in the face of the just man he would sentence to death, and in an act of symbolic innocence, washed his hands.

"I am free of the blood of this just man; see you to it."

Then answered all the people, "His blood be on us and on our children."

Then he released Barabbas unto them, and when he had scourged Jesus, he delivered him to be crucified. Then the soldiers of the governor took Jesus into the Praetorium and gathered unto Him the whole garrison of soldiers. And they stripped Him and put on Him a scarlet robe. And when they had platted a crown of thorns, they put it upon His head, and a reed in His right hand, and they bowed the knee before Him, and mocked Him, saying, "Hail, King of the Jews!"

And they spat on Him, and took the reed and smote Him on the head. After they had mocked Him, they took the robe off Him, and put His own raiment on Him, then led Him away to crucify Him. And as they came out, they found a man of Cyrene, Simon by name; him they compelled to bear Yeshua's cross. (Matthew 27:25-32).

The brutality preceding the crucifixion intensified beyond the hall called the Praetorium. The *Verdict of the Shroud* documents cuts and bruises all over Jesus' body: gashes where His beard was plucked out and puncture wounds with a swollen abdomen that led to His eventual asphyxiation. Jesus became an unsightly picture of human torture. The beating injured His blood vessels and soft tissue, causing blood to leak from the broken capillaries and become trapped under His skin. Severe punctures with dumbbell-shaped markings from the Roman whip, peppered the entire body.

The flagrum, which is the Roman whip, is weighted at its tips with particles of sharpened bone or lead. The Roman soldiers were given the honor of scourging Jesus with the flagrum while He was bent over a whipping post. Ninety to 120 gashes in Jesus' flesh have been counted on the Shroud of Turin. A three-pronged whip and forty lashes, as mentioned in the Scriptures, calculate accurately that which has been reported. The severity of the scourging helped hasten Jesus' death. The beating caused internal hemorrhaging in the chest cavity, resulting in a buildup of a bloody mix of serum-water and blood, which led to His suffocation. When the Roman soldier pierced Jesus's side to see if He was already dead, the bloody mix of blood and water gushed out. (John 19:34).

And when they came to the place called Golgotha, that is to say, a place of a skull, they gave Him vinegar to drink mingled with gall. When He had tasted it, He would not drink. And they crucified Him, and parted His garments, casting lots, that it might be fulfilled which was spoken by the prophet, "They parted My garments among them, and upon My vesture they cast lots." Then, sitting down, they watched Him and set up over His head His accusation written, This Is Jesus, The King of The Jews. (Matthew 27:33–36).

Every man can take comfort in Jesus's crucifixion. Jesus offered His life and His blood as payment for any sin man will ever commit by enduring the ultimate torture that any man can ever face. Not only so, but those who ask for His sacrifice to be applied to their sin, become spiritually free of the penalty and the punishment for their sin. A lamb without sin, blemish, spot, or wrinkle was offered freely as a sacrifice for those who err at the call. In the beginning, sin entered the world by one man, Adam; therefore, it is justified that by one man, Jesus Christ, there is an offering of righteousness for all.

Man's incompetence to match the wiles of the Devil made it necessary for Christ to confront and destroy the power of evil that rules the heart of man. After he died, Jesus made His way down to Hell to confront His greatest rival. There was much work to be done in Hell. The first order of business was to take back the key of life, which Adam gave up in the garden of Eden. The second business was to give a second chance to the souls who had lost their way in life. Jesus had an evangelistic church service in Hell.

"Come to Me, all whose hearts are broken and contrite before God. I have paid the price for your sins. If you believe, break free of your chains and come to Me." Jesus entered the domain of Hell and stripped the authority that bound man to sin.

Who else could have loosed the seal of death? Who else knows the secrets of Hell? Who else could have been chosen to fight the enemy of God? Who else could have been offered as a blood sacrifice to pay for and redeem the life of man? (Revelation 5).

What has Jehovah God done for His people? He provided an escape from the hordes of Hell. Man has an escape by simply accepting the offering of the blood of His Son Jesus, the Christ. Did Christ offer a solution to earthly dictatorship, the control of leaders who push men into oppression? Yes, He did. He empowered man beyond his physical ability to defeat the hosts of darkness that swarm the Earth with manifestations of evil.

And the dictator within, the ever-brewing taste for it all? Where shall I run? To battle with that which I cannot see is hopeless. The battle that cannot be seen by physical eyes has the capacity to strangle the heart and spirit of man and shackle him to unimaginable darkness. Lurking in the shadows of the heart are the destructive and shameful patterns of our own lives. We have learned to shove them in the closets of time, with the hope they will be on their best behavior when we turn on the lights. The trouble is, they are true to their designs; shame and destruction waft around their prey like thick clouds of monsters, which choke out the sweetness of life, if not for the blood of Jesus Christ.

12

The Covenant of Marriage

A key to solving life's mystery of success.

The covenant of marriage is designed to begin with the shedding of blood, which becomes a holy bond to be shared between a man and his wife. The wife presents a virtuous body to her husband, and a holy covenant is cut and sealed between them: a matrimonial intimacy where the man and the woman ultimately become one.

The shedding of blood in the covenant of marriage elevates the institution of marriage from a mere earthly agreement to a spiritual knot—the making of two individuals into one. Therefore, marriage is holy, and because it is holy, it is also sacred, which means every marriage is a covenant connected to God. This unique bonding could only have been designed by our Creator. It is the only covenant on Earth where the body speaks its own excited language in flames of emotional and physical tones.

Behind the mystery and excitement of two separate individuals becoming one is a most powerful purpose. This is where marriage becomes divine. The reason God gave man the plan of marriage is so that he would never be alone in his spiritual battle. But the plot thickens. Not only can the man take a wife to stand beside him on his journey through life, but the man and his wife are also able to produce an army—their very own defense force. No, the battle plan does not stop there. When the couple produces children, the children become the fiercest warriors during their innocence. Even before the child can sound out words, the cooing and the baby talk are equal to wielding swords in the spirit.

Out of the mouth of babies and those who are not yet weaned from the breast, God commands strength to silence any enemy or those who would seek to do the family harm. (Psalm 8:2).

The purpose of marriage is to build an army; an army that builds a community, a community that builds a city, and a city that builds a nation. Marriage is the building of nations that are equipped with supernatural powers—a united force to destroy God's enemy. Success in marriage is the ability to preserve the sweet love and harmony when the enemy comes to destroy the nation. When the man and his wife fiercely protect the dream of unity and the purity of radical love, it opens the gateway of life as life was meant to be.

Virtue is the foundation on which this covenant is built. Making the case for purity before entering into marriage in our present culture, seems more of an insult than a protection of the truth. The honor of virtue is a precious gift that must be reserved for the marriage bed. What better gift can a husband present to his wife than the gift of having reserved his intimacy for her alone? Society protects itself when it waves red flags of warning for impurity. The rumor mill of gossip for the suspected young girl who seems to be passing out her jewels seemed like a cruel joke, but it played its part in preserving virgins. It should not be easy for precious virgins to be taken or handed over as cheaply as candy. Fathers must stand as brick walls between predators and their precious daughters.

The thief comes and steals the heart, steals time, and steals intimacy: the thief cheapens marriages. The thief sits and plans for days, months, or even years how it will win over the heart and the time that belongs to the marriage so as to create a breach in the intimacy. This destructive plan is overlaid with gold and dazzles the eyes of the victim because it targets the weakness of the marriage. The thieves of marriages are like viruses; once they insert themselves into the host, the infection begins spreading and causes damage to the organs—to the children, the finances, the happiness, and the strength of the marriage. Because the infection has secured itself inside the host, the marriage has no choice but to begin destroying itself from within. The truth is, many of the viruses were introduced before the marriage began. Additionally, the demise may begin with husband and wife, but like a forest fire, it will spread its fangs from the children of the union down through generations.

Just as viruses make the body diseased and miserable, there are various actions and attitudes that must never be part of a marriage. Conflict—fighting without intending to find a solution—is a bitter disease to pour into marriage. Conflict breeds disgust because dark words have a poisonous sting. Unkind words are like bee stings; they pile on top of each other and, sooner rather than later, send the mind into shock. One word can trigger the shock that sends the tongue on a wild ride. This tongue-lashing behavior defends itself by making enemies of those who do not approve. To control its enemies, the mind, which is living in shock-mode, plans all sorts of make-believe, double-dealing pretenses. To juggle shock-mode and double-dealing, is too much of a balancing act. It leaves the mind wasted and lonely, craving and accepting attention from sources that have no pleasure. Strange, that the one who was the mastermind at sustaining conflict has become the court jester for a king whose heart is stone cold. Bad decisions create conflict, conflict breeds disgust, disgust entertains lies, lies are kissing cousins with lust, lust is driven by brokenness, and brokenness is the product of impurity.

Like father, like son. Monkey see, monkey do. The apple doesn't fall far from the tree. These clichés have long existed to prove that generational curses are kept alive within families. We call them curses but never stop to examine their beginnings. Plus, if a family member tries to break the mold, somehow it triggers a sense of intolerance. People we love and care for suddenly become enemies, and from our souls gush distaste strong enough to produce lifelong adversaries.

Who wins? No one. What do we gain? Absolutely nothing. However, the pressure within the soul to keep the differences alive is rock solid. It seems easier to gossip or speak negatively than to compliment or celebrate someone's achievement. Instead of watching over and caring for the vulnerable, we sit comfortably on the stool of doom and gloom, then peddle the news of failure when trouble takes its toll. It is easy to gloat when others fall if there is no love in the soul. Love, is taught: enjoying other people's misfortune, is taught; and watching someone fall into the ditch without covering the hole, is taught. Life lessons are taught while we grow together as families. Once we understand that these lessons benefit no one, we must unlearn them and drag the mind to the school of compassion.

No one benefits from other people's failure, but it takes time to prove that true. Immediate gratifications are not blessings. Blessings are sustained rewards sent from God, and they touch people, places, and things, bringing so much joy and prosperity that they become contagious.

If someone is hurting, I must take the time to walk alongside them and help pull them out of the path of pain. That is the only way to do life. Genuine love does not stand alone; it builds an army of warriors: warriors who were destined to fall but were set free by love.

In a broken home, where vows have been replaced by the cruelty of unkind words and the lies that breed harmful actions, the first-line recipients are usually the children. This is how it works. When the covenant of love is broken, it invites dark, ugly thoughts that push everyone into fighting mode. These actions are only introduced after a particular incident. This incident could be a simple smile from someone who is so desperate for attention, they could not care less who gets hurt while they are on the hunt. These attention flags have a sinkhole and pull their victims away from true love and family. The sinkhole is like the rabbit trail of Alice in Wonderland, full of leads but goes nowhere. When the victim returns from isolation to reality, the covenant of marriage looks like rat bait—all that's left are the crumbs.

The spirit of brokenness uses lies to isolate at least one person in the covenant. Then it removes the covering needed to protect the ones who are in danger. The weaker ones are exposed to the greater danger, while the stronger are usually insensitive to the truth. A person who is broken inside does not wrestle with truth, because the mind has been rewired to defend the chase of the sinkhole.

Soon, the spirit of brokenness invites emptiness. Emptiness has a trapdoor that pulls on those who wander close to its den. It is vast, and dark, and lonely; reaping, yet offering nothing. The longer it keeps its victims, the more it takes. The backdoor of those who are empty leads to a search for fulfillment not only for the adults but also for the children. For example, a young girl with an absentee father spends her entire life searching for a father to fill the gap. The search is a fantasy because she does not have the map or the true picture to find the treasure. No one can find that which has no identity. During this chase, there are periods of testing where she pauses long enough to find out if *this catch* is father material or not. Moving on is not unusual, because each protégée must be like the father in her mind, flaws and all, or he has failed the test. Since the father was absent, she can handle a catch who has another family. Since love is a feeling, she will build the relationship on moments of happiness. Since the fling must be riddled with bullets of fighting, she must move on to the next catch, because nothing satisfies. As she moves on, her heart becomes more detached and increasingly angry. Let's not mention the baggage she incurs as the journey progresses. If that journey includes giving birth to a child, she becomes the ingrained role model for that youngster's life.

Young boys from broken homes find comfort in roaming and filling time with creative mischief. Interestingly, a man never feels comfortable staying where chaos exists unless he is the author of it. Another amazing observation is that young boys find comfort in numbers, and instinctively, a leader emerges. This leader takes the group to the edge and earns the sought-after respect men give to trailblazers. Excitement builds, and brotherhood is born. Ripping him from the hood is like taking another family member from his life, because these members intrigue his fantasy. A wife who eventually finds the ticket to his heart, or is admitted to his fan club, becomes married to his shadow. His interest in the marriage is divided. He sees the marriage as a conquest—he went to war, beat back his enemies, and walked away the victor with a beautiful bride on his arm. Now that the war is over, he spends time inventing ways to keep this fresh kill alive. It's like a cat with a mouse. The cat is only interested as long as the mouse is alive. A young boy who is broken inside becomes a player who wants no responsibility. The relationship must continue to stimulate him, always taking him to the edge. Without the stimulus, freedom seems like a greater pleasure than the legacy his wife can help him build. A wife given the task of holding him in the marriage becomes a magician in her own right.

Wives of broken marriages experience the gut-wrenching spirit of disappointment. The walk down the aisle was filled with a lifetime of expectations. Most women did not walk down the aisle because they were loved, but because they were given the promise. Once she becomes wife, she puts on her construction boots and begins shoveling to build the empire. A wife sees love as an appreciation of the value she brings to the table. Value could be her physical beauty, or it could be a sacrifice she makes in the marriage. Wherever she sees her worth, she will begin building on it. The breakdown of the marriage for the woman usually comes when the husband does not celebrate her worth. If his reason for wanting to be married was to have a household maid or a bearer of children, it does not matter how hard she tries, her efforts for love will go unnoticed. A wife whose expectations are unmet and whose efforts are ignored becomes bitter.

Even if the woman produced the folly that created the downward spiral of the relationship, she continuously questions the sincerity of the husband who did not understand her sacrifice. She sees his lack of understanding as a betrayal rather than a lack of wisdom. As a mother, she is not careful to watch over her daughter and guide her diligently out of the path of predators—exploiters who seek to reduce her to a notch in the belt and the gratification of a sick mind. As she becomes absorbed in her torturous misfortune, the signs and cries for attention from her daughter are misinterpreted and blend with her sorrows as part of the package of failure. For her son, it becomes a welcomed solution that he finds comfort elsewhere, as her bosom of love has dried up. Without even trying, she begins to disrespect her husband. She becomes a teacher of psychology and spends her days planning her lessons. These are the lessons she hopes will drive him to his knees before her ladyship so that she can declare herself successful in the business of conquering her man.

It is the glory of a man to stand tall, and to stand tall, he must believe he is free—truly free. A man who is under the thumb of his bride will release his body from the grip yet leave his ghost so she will believe she is still in charge. Husbands hide pain and a lack of fulfillment in crafts that make them feel powerful. In this marriage, it was his desire to create a stage, a castle from which he could shine. That's what the world expected of him, and he had every intention of doing it. However, he was upstaged, and his ability or his window of interest to build the shrine was destroyed. Not to mention, the joy of recreating the castle is stolen. But true to his manly nature, he will rise again, especially in the public's eye. The power to rise is derived from the strangest of modes. Power could be the merciless blows he uses to defend his honor when he feels the collapse of his world. Power could be the next world empire that rises from rubble. Power could be the high from drugs, alcohol, and the like, true to the old, old tale that they numb the pain.

The beneficiaries of destroyed marriage vows are not family members. That which enjoys this trip has got to be the spirit of brokenness or the spirit of impurity. Too many subtle unpleasantries that rob the love and joy of family are introduced to make a broken marriage a mere intolerance of behavior or irreconcilable differences. Division, not separation, is enough ground for contrary spirits to thrive. Father tearing in one direction, mother tugging in another, kids running wild, wolves stealing precious lives. We must see that in it all, there are spirits—spirits of lust, spirits of jealousy, spirits of theft, spirits of deceit, spirits of torment, spirits of maliciousness, spirits of greed, sickness, death... and the list goes on. It does not take a stretch of the imagination to realize that unwanted intrusions lead to immorality, which leaves scarred instead of virtuous women and men for future generations.

But quietly, very quietly, someone or something is cashing in on it all. Take off your shoes—shhh. Please, on your tippy toes, follow me. Let's go to the attic; I want to show you something. Close your eyes; now open them. Look! See the smoke of intoxication oozing from the pipes of death? Smell the putrid air of sulfur mixed with the foul smell of decay—the smell of rotting flesh. Look around at your feet; see the wet and clammy crawling creatures like miniature worms? Now, let your eyes focus through the thick blackness. Can you see the oversized, black, venomous creatures at the table, enjoying this party? This is their home now; they rule from here.

Somehow, it must be possible to step beyond the natural into the world that controls mankind. Perhaps we would not be so hard-hearted and unfeeling if we could see each other's brokenness. What if we could see the spirits at work in our loved ones, would we fight for them? We see the drunken stupor of husbands or wives as they give themselves over to rage and vile outbursts that send shock waves through the house and frighten everyone into subjection. At times, we feel sickness overwhelm our bodies, taking its toll, especially on our ability to make conscious decisions. We become too weak to concentrate; the brain feels like it has turned to mush.

But perhaps the deadliest fuels that feed these dark, ugly spirits are the words of death we speak. Curse words are the language of hell. They have the power to call up slime of the darkest order and set it to work in our lives. Profanity is the only language where the same words have a different meaning every time they are spoken. That's the language of the spirits of hell, and we empower the hordes of death every time we sound off. When we speak curses, we are calling on hell to come and perform acts of evil in our homes.

Some of the grossest sins we commit are done in the privacy of our homes. Surely, a man's home is his temple. There, we are free to speak our minds. We bring to our homes the fruits of our labor. We decorate as lavishly or as carelessly as we choose, and it becomes the resting place of many of our earthly treasures. We are our true selves at home; there are no cover-ups, our guards are down, and our imaginations are unleashed. Outside the home, we portray the image we want the public to perceive. Occasionally, we slip, and the truth gushes out, but home is reality. Let's face it, when our homes are not sanctified, our lives are chaotic. When the sanctification of the blood of the Lord Jesus Christ is completed in our homes, God will execute a mighty deliverance. Marriage is built on God, and God wants to become one with our pain, our joys, and our family.

Love—not tolerance or fear—true love can save any marriage. Love takes the fight into the chamber of God and begs for His hand of mercy. Love brings back the gift of mercy and washes the house of the filth and muck that has begun to grow. Love goes back to the chamber of God and implores His hand for grace. Grace is used to refurbish and decorate. Again, love travels to the portals of Heaven, but this time, it enters the courts of truth; it stays a while as a case is made. This time, the petition is more demanding; it wants the Presence of the Most High God.

To return with the Spirit of God necessitates a host of angels bearing the Word of truth, righteousness, peace, and forgiveness. The angels must carry the instruments needed to mend and put hearts back together. They will come into the home and build a spiritual operating room. This is no small task. To enter the courts of the Almighty, there must be thanksgiving and worship. The heart must be filled with the warm-and-fuzzies of thankfulness because the Spirit of God is like a magnet to a warm heart. The return trip is expected to meet with great opposition. The attic has been cleaned, but the spirits are lurking, waiting for an opportunity to return. If they see heavenly reinforcement, there will be an all-out war.

A decision is made. Love will go back to the home and mount a defense of prayer for seven days. During this time, different angels will be dispatched to bring the request, bit by bit. Truth will be first; it will come in tiny doses. Forgiveness will follow. Forgiveness is hated by the spirits of darkness, and they seem to detect it from miles away. Forgiveness must be wrapped in love if it will ever have a chance to succeed. Love has to carefully watch for it and vow to help protect its safe arrival. If only we could see life as it spiritually is.

The ability to regain the wholesomeness and beauty in marriage rests on forgiveness and truth. In order for repentance to take place, there needs to be a forgiving heart. Forgiveness breeds repentance. Repentance to sin is like radiation to cancer—it shrivels and shrivels until it dies. Remission of the cancer of sin is the most powerful gift we can produce in marriage. Husband and wife become vulnerable and open without anger and without bitterness. Truth is a spiritual detergent; it washes and sanitizes everything spotlessly. Forgiveness is the ointment for healing. A clean wound will eventually heal, but an ointment hastens the process. The next step is the reinstatement of the covenant. This time, the covenant is cut and solidified with the blood of the Lord Jesus Christ, the third party and keeper of the covenant of marriage.

Restoration of the covenant comes through cleansing. As intended by God, this exclusive bond, shared by man and wife, is similar to the covenant Christ made with the Church. Christ entered into a covenant with His bride, the Church, by laying down His life for the Church so He might sanctify and cleanse it with the washing of water by the Word of God. (Ephesians 5:23–30). Really, Christ made provision to keep the Church as His pure and undefiled possession. Christ knew that the spiritual soap of the Word was always going to be needed for His Church because the devil would always be sneaking in with impurities.

Impurities break covenants. Once undesirables, foreign matters, and not-part-of-the-covenant particles enter the marriage, it begins to fall apart. Therefore, there remains a never-ending source of cleansing for the bride of Christ. If she continues to wash herself with the word of God, she will not fall prey to the traps that beget impurity.

Covenants are symbolic of protection. God told Israel to eat the Passover in their houses—the houses where the lambs were kept. The place where the Lamb of God is kept and where the blood of the Lamb is shed becomes sacred. That which is sacred is connected to

God. Next, God told His children to spread the blood over all the entrances. Do not be ashamed of the cleansing blood; make it part of the covenant of the home. Passover is the instruction God has given to protect and sanctify our homes. The communion of Passover is the answer to driving out the works of unrighteousness from our sacred place and making them holy unto the Lord.

13

Dabbling

Blessed be the name of God forever.
Wisdom and might are His
and He changes times and seasons. Daniel 2:20-21

This business of life has mesmerized us all. It seems failure has its nose in everybody's business. Study the details, follow the plans, stick to the disciplines; but at some point along that path, failure shows up, flips the script, and everyone has to sit back and watch it demolish years of hard work. No one can prepare for this phase of life because it is the unforeseen, the unpredictable, the unknown. Some believe that failure and its nosy business can be erased by tapping into the magic of the spirit world. After all, blood is the currency that is offered to the spirit world in exchange for favors. If failure comes knocking, make a sacrifice of blood and drive it away. True, but there are details to using the currency; the spirit world is not just a trick of the mind.

The Earth is full of principles that teach us how to approach the spirit world. A woman is pregnant, a baby is being formed in her womb, and without fail, we know what to expect at the time of birth. "Boy or girl?" She will never give birth to a cat or a fish. Crossed species cannot make it to term because the body cannot tolerate the mixing of genes. The immune system is the watchdog of the body, and it does not compromise. If the genes of the cat or the fish were mixed and inserted into her womb, abortion would be automatic. Therefore, a kangaroo cannot give birth to a fly, and humans cannot give birth to whales. Just as there are principles to the body's function, so there are spiritual watchdogs to the use of blood. The mixing of crossed-up ideas of the truth of the spirit world creates spiritual abortions.

In the religions of the world, theories abound. Every religion states its history and origin with stories of earthly gods and spiritual contacts (more or less). The universal train of thought is that religion offers hope and answers to the abnormal challenges of life. When life throws a curve-ball that breaks the soul, instead of becoming anxious or falling apart, most people turn to God and find comfort. The trouble is that religion is complex and hard to understand. How can one accurately find the truth? The best answer is to combine all the religious beliefs and then rest in the assurance that somewhere in it all lies the answer. However, that theory is full of holes, because no one can righteously serve many gods. It is far too complicated to follow multiple trails all at the same time. Therefore, because religion is the answer to solving the failures of life, there is an absolute need for choice. Here comes the task of religious abortion. If the body is equipped with such a wonderful system of casting out that which is destructive, the mind will be even more powerful. Deep within the subconscious lies the wisdom that filters out the things that are not good for the soul.

If religion were unnecessary, it would never have become a concern for every single person. Many people have heard of the Amazon jungle, but how many care about it or that it exists? Not so with religion; it rings in the subconscious. *Easy, the answers have got to be easy; it just feels like I am missing a basic, simple truth.* This necessary requirement tugs at the soul of man, crying and calling for attention, sometimes even more than our basic needs. Religion becomes especially important when someone close to our hearts dies.

Death is a cruel reminder of how unsteady this tightrope walk of life truly is. The soul mourns with waves of sadness, shared in common grief. The heart is weakened because death is decorated with the bow of failure. No matter how great and successful a man becomes, death will tear him down to the grave. The strongest barriers that have stood many moons against failure lower themselves without question when staring at the grave. Death seems to laugh in the face of uncertainty with mockery and insults that become unbearable. Those who witness this hopelessness cry out with agony, perhaps more so out of knowing that the clock is ticking.

The searching of the soul for an escape from death has led the Earth through a maze of answers. Depending on who presents the answer, or how the answer is presented, we dabble to find comfort from the sorrows of life and from death. It is in the face of these insecurities that man has conjured what can be called the *God complex*. With the God complex, man makes up a story to solve the spiritual puzzles of life. Astrology has paved the path for spells, hexes, and magic. Dabbling in these crafts has opened the doors to otherworldly experiences that bring a daring hope of conquering the unknown. The invitation to explore and go beyond takes the soul to new heights. It hands power to the enchanter, levels of power far beyond natural abilities. Those who dabble in magic are given remedies that seem to bring a measure of ease to trouble. To be counted worthy of receiving these remedies, the seeker must pay a grand price. The exchange is brutal because the price must include blood, and to become successful, it must also include the soul. A hush is breathed over the process because everyone knows this kind of tampering is taboo. However, when we become desperate, the mind will push the limits of acceptance and belief, as this kind of dabbling seems to be the only answer.

Dabbling is a gamble. To make it attractive and to remove the high possibility that it may not work, we are warned that it only works when we believe. Everyone is told that the degree to which we believe determines whether the spells will cook up on the right side. That is easy to understand because Jesus Christ told His followers that they had to believe that His blood would speak to God on their behalf. The spirit world works if we believe. The difference between dabbling in spells and incantations compared to the blood of Jesus Christ is that Christ will rescue those who sincerely call on Him. For those who dabble in witchcraft, the responsibility of success is removed from the enchanter and placed on the belief of the seeker. If the spell did not work, it is only because the seeker did not truly believe. But in the recesses of our souls, we know the truth. We know that blood sacrifices of incantations call up the dark forces of evil to work. Since they have no allegiance to anything or anyone, it becomes a toss-up as to whether or not they will honor the covenant. Not to mention that calling on the forces of evil means the package comes with evil.

These are disturbing thoughts we must ponder. Spirits are not bound by the laws that humans must obey. When a spirit is present, it can move objects without being seen, and it can whisper ideas to the mind: spirits are not limited to what they can do on the Earth. Anyone who chooses to play in this danger zone knows the risks. The stakes are high and the cost astronomical, because those who dabble must also pay with their minds. After weighing the risks, we must convince ourselves that it is worth the price. Hail to the day that the requests become granted, for that was all we needed to unboggle the mind. But then reality strikes, and strikes ruthlessly, when death, like a loathsome dragon, rears its ugly head and deals its fatal blow. Then the seeker is back to the drawing board, because there is no comfort for those who dabble.

Some people are born with a spiritual touch. They will have dreams or strong sensations when something weird is about to happen. In the Book of Matthew, the angel of the Lord appeared to Joseph through a dream and told him to take his young child and wife and flee to the safety of Egypt, as the child was in danger of being killed.

Sleep is the uncontrolled state the body enters, and in this mode, it becomes a sort of death-like experience. It is in this state of lack of control that dreams are produced. Yes, dreams come from another world which we enter during sleep. To complicate matters, that which we see in our dreams sometimes plays out in real life. Dreams are proof that life will continue after death. Sleep takes us into that afterlife world and speaks to us daily, asking us to listen, asking us to pay attention. Man enters the spirit world every time he sleeps, and he is actively a part of that world. Every man has evidence that a world exists that is out of his control, and we enter that world is when the body goes into that death-like mode of sleep.

Those who remember and can interpret their dreams are able to control their future. God uses dreams to forewarn man of the plans of darkness against his life. The dream takes us to the scene as it is taking place in the spirit world. Our Father God allows us to see the trouble before it is played out in the Earth. Once we see it, we have the power to abort the plan before it comes into the Earth. Dreams are God's way of empowering His children to win the war against evil. The activities we see in our dreams are canceled by the prayers we send up to God. When we ask in prayer, God releases His angels to cancel the plans before they get sent to the Earth.

Daniel answered in the presence of the king and said, "The secret that the king has demanded cannot be shown to the king by the wise men, the astrologers, the magicians, or the soothsayers. But there is a God in heaven that reveals secrets, and makes known to the king Nebuchadnezzar what shall be in the latter days. The dream and the visions of your head upon your bed are these: as for you, O king, your thoughts came into your mind upon your bed about what should come to pass hereafter, and He that reveals secrets makes known to you what shall come to pass. (Daniel 2:27–29).

Life is the sum of dreams and thoughts and how we allow them to play out in our lives. If we cannot imagine it, then we won't get excited about it. We will never be driven to fulfill dreams that our minds cannot plan. Everything we achieve in life, we first become passionate about. The story of our lives tells the actions we have prioritized. Then there were things we believed in so much, we practiced them repeatedly. These were the ideas that became habits because they brought happiness. It is true that practice becomes perfect; the more we dabble, the better we become. The more power we gain, the more irresistible the craft. The more power we find, the greater the level of surrender. The greater the level of surrender, the weaker the mind becomes.

For your heavenly Father knows that you have need of all these things. But seek first the kingdom of God and His righteousness, and all these things shall be added unto you. (Matthew 6:32–33).

It is amazing that in just one book, all the answers to life can be found. God is not asking us to hide our eyes from the spirit world; the opposite is true. God is inviting us to taste the joys of Heaven while we are alive on Earth. Man must tap into the spiritual realm, or his soul will never be satisfied or accomplished.

No author has walked away and chosen not to be identified with the greatness of a published work. No farmer has seen his crops ready for harvest, then abandoned his hard labor and left them to die. No designer being praised for the uniqueness of a new concept denies his work. It is not possible that the Creator would deny access to the created, for God designed man that they both would fellowship together. God is recruiting worshipers, and the only requirement is that they worship Him in Spirit and in truth. God will never turn away from those who seek Him with their whole hearts.

God chooses to insert Himself in His children's failure to write the ultimate comeback story. The offer is extended to dabble with the Holy Spirit—better known as the Presence of God. We start with truth—an acknowledgment of who we are and where we have been. Next, we align ourselves with the holiness of God and invite our Creator to touch our lives again. We become intrigued by the fellowship and enticed by the possibilities of the Almighty so that it becomes a weakness—a passion. We sit at the feet of love and allow God's beauty to unravel, because the reward of dabbling with the Almighty God is eternal life.

14

Role of the Holy Spirit

They who are led by the Spirit of God, are sons of God. Romans 8:14

When Jesus Christ was leaving Heaven, he packed a number of different gifts in the suitcase He brought to Earth. Before He unpacked the suitcase, He searched for the right people with whom He could leave the treasures. If He left the gifts with the right individuals, the gifts would multiply and eventually fill the Earth. Once the gifts filled the Earth, the Earth would begin to function just like Heaven, and people's lives would become beautiful.

A gift that Jesus brought, which must not be ignored, is the giving of the Holy Spirit. As different as we all are, so are our opinions. As we study the Bible or search for the truth and revelation of our Father God, each person is apt to use experience, social upbringing, and biases to interpret God. Eventually, God would become known as a patchwork of people's opinions. To avoid that catastrophe, God sent the gift of the Holy Spirit with His son, Jesus Christ. Those who accept the gift of the Holy Spirit have the privilege of being schooled in the ways and means of Heaven. As they gain knowledge, the Holy Spirit adds power to the knowledge, and greatness begins to unfold. Men use the Holy Spirit to become successful in their God-given destiny. By allowing the Holy Spirit to teach and guide their lives, they remove the limits from life and become supernatural in their endeavors.

Jesus exposed the power of the Holy Spirit to His disciples in doses. One day, He sat them down for a test. The focus of the quiz was to determine if the disciples could identify the power and activity from Heaven when it came into the Earth. Peter got it right. He said, "Jesus, You have been sent from God. You are the son of the living God."

At that point, Jesus knew Peter had emerged as a leader of the disciples. The Holy Spirit had connected Peter with the Father, and Peter's responses to life were not based on emotions or biases. Peter had begun to talk with the Father God, and to listen to His heart. This was done through the work of the Holy Spirit.

Flesh and blood did not reveal this to you, Peter, but My Father who is in Heaven. Upon the seeking and pursuing of the truth of God, upon those who know and follow the path of the Holy Spirit, I will issue Heaven's power. I will build My Church, and the gates of Hell shall not prevail. And I will give to you the keys of the Kingdom of Heaven, and whatsoever you bind on Earth will be bound in Heaven, and whatsoever you loose on Earth will be loosed in Heaven. (Matthew 16:13–19).

Jesus was not issuing keys to the kingdom of Earth, but to the kingdom of Heaven. The kingdom of Heaven is the seat and the gate of earthly activities. It all begins at the spiritual gates. To grasp this concept, we need to be introduced to the world called the Heavens and then learn to live in it. Followers of Christ are given the gift of the Presence of God, whom we refer to as the Holy Spirit, and He ushers them in and becomes their guide.

In Paul's first letter to the Corinthians, he engaged them in a mystery. Those who have found the Holy Spirit speak the wisdom of God with words that seem like foolishness. This wisdom has been hidden from the rulers of the ages. Had the princes of this world known the spiritual plans that were set in place for the Earth, they would not have crucified the Lord of Glory. But they were blinded, and their hearts were tricked because they had been given a sense of false power. They were tricked into believing they were holding spiritual and earthly power in their hands when they crucified the Christ. Paul discovered that wisdom which results in glory, has been hidden by God, and revealed to those who choose to accept the gift of His Holy

Spirit. For the Spirit searches out the deep things of the heart of God and teaches them to the ones who are diligent.

As Paul said to the Corinthian Church, "No one knows the heart of another man. Only an individual can claim to truly know who he or she is." So it is with the Holy Spirit. Just acknowledging God does not make us privy to the Spirit of God. The relationship must be real, and the fellowship has to become intimate. When the heart is invested, God grants His Presence so that we may know Him. The mystery is that this cannot be done in our own understanding. Man can only know God by His Spirit. The uniting of God and man is a lifelong investment that produces treasures of knowledge. The return on this investment is wisdom, which analyzes the state of the Earth then matches it with the plans of Heaven to produce legacies. This free flow of the God-knowledge and wisdom confuses the minds of those who have no access to its depth. Not until it is displayed in the Earth and produces never-before-experienced events can others perceive the depth of the experience that came from the Spirit of God. Through the Holy Spirit, we are given the mind of Christ.

All things are of God, are made by God, and serve the purposes of God. Therefore, the Holy Spirit takes us through the spiritual realm on a discovery of the vastness of God. The Holy Spirit is the promise of the Father given to the saints to explore the treasures of Heaven. The saints gain access to the Holy Spirit when they become born again. To be born again, they become completely submitted to God the Father with full acceptance of His son, Jesus Christ. Jesus explained it to Nicodemus, the Jewish ruler, by saying, "First be baptized in water to wash away and bury past sins. Next, ask God for the gift of the Holy Spirit. Anyone who sincerely asks for the Holy Spirit will not be denied." Those who become born again begin a spiritual journey, a journey of the Heavens. The ride through the realms of the spirit is a complete vision of the facets of Heaven and Earth. The born again are successful in the Earth because they have discovered the treasures of the Heavens.

In 1 Corinthians 12, the writings explain how the Holy Spirit perfects those who desire to be holy. Holy is the term used for those who fall in love with the Holy Spirit. Holy Spirit lovers are perfected through the bonding of spiritual power. Man does not have to settle for counterfeit power, or calling on dumb idols, or tapping into the next best thing when he has the Presence of God. The Holy Spirit ensures profits by distributing gifts of all kinds for any situation man may face. Ultimately, man becomes so powerful, he attains the wealth, the inheritance, and the holiness of Christ.

Let's explore God's gift of miracles, prophecy, and tongues. Miracles are expressions of the spirit realm seen on Earth by physical eyes. They are a supernatural display for human benefit. Miracles violate Earth's laws but give joy to the heart of man. Healing is a miracle where the Holy Spirit gives man the ability to speak over dead or dying cells and bring them back to life. The gift of prophecy is used to predict and change the future. Prophecy is not a wish list that comes to life because someone was daring enough to ask for it. A prophet is one who knows and speaks about events that will take place, events that will change the world. The prophet's heart is tapped into the heart of God, God reveals the future, and the prophet makes it known long before the event occurs.

Tongues are most interesting. Many Christians have placed this gift on the back burner, and some have hoped it would disintegrate. It has been ridiculed, contradicted, dubbed a foolishness of the mind, and more. However, tongues are simply the language of God. We speak the language of our native tongue, and a stranger is awed by its fluency and someone else's understanding of it. So it is with the man who navigates the spiritual realm through the Holy Spirit; he speaks the language of God fluently. At first, tongues are just an exciting language that flows when the Spirit of God is busy at work in the mind. The more the Spirit is given access to the mind, the more the language of Heaven is expressed. The speaker does not seek to understand, because it becomes a sweet acknowledgment of the Presence of God. However, the closer the relationship becomes, the greater the understanding of tongues. When the Holy Spirit begins to reveal the words of this supernatural gift, the heart hears prayers, wise counsel, and knowledge from the heart of God.

Take a ride with me through the Heavens. Angels of God are ushering us through the realms of the spirit. In the book of Ephesians, Paul tells us we are seated in heavenly places in Christ. This ride through the Heavens is taking us to our seat of heavenly authority. The Holy Spirit, the Presence of God, is our guide, and as we see and experience new dimensions, we become awed by the splendor and glory of it all. Then, in heavenly language, we begin to adore the awesomeness of our Father God, and the native language of heaven rolls off our tongues. Worship flows to the Most High, who was, and is, and is to come.

It is easy to see that love is twisted, and tied, and knotted up with spiritual gifts. When we have experienced God in His majestic glory, the troubles, or pleasures, or frowns of life lose their impact on our souls. The grip and struggle with sin fade away in the light of the experience of God's holy Presence. Love will never fail us. Love will never cause the bottom to fall out. Love never gives the wrong advice, or causes our hearts to hold onto a grudge, or agrees with the pain of unforgiveness. Love writes a story that leads us directly to the promise of success. A promise that never fails because we are perfected with just a glimpse of the magnificence of love—for there is no failure in God.

Lost in the beauty of God's grace, captured by the sweetness of His voice, and mesmerized by the tenderness of the moment, earthly achievements pale, words fail, and homage is reduced to "Holy, holy, holy; the Lord our God is holy."

15

Covenant Communion Passover

This is the day of my new beginning!

The Lord God instituted an ordinance for His people, Israel, to forever destroy the lifelong yoke that stifled them as a nation. So powerful was the ordinance that it generated what became known as the Exodus; and yes, the ordinance was signed in blood. Every family had its own personal experience with the shedding of the blood of a lamb without blemish; then the blood was slathered on the doors and lintels of their homes. Blood was the sign of protection each family proudly displayed in obedience to God's word. That night, the angel of death would pass through town, and when he saw the blood, he would not enter that house.

In every house without blood, the firstborn was taken. The ache of death was heard far and wide as sorrow was poured out on those without the covering of blood. That which became a great deliverance for the weak was a double-edged sword for the strong. Therefore, it was not difficult for the protected to remember yearly the impact and significance of the passing over of death. This must have been a sacred celebration, with each person recounting an exclusive yet similar story—how, by obedience to the Word of God, they were spared.

Years later, Jesus Christ came to Earth and completed the final phase of this significant ordinance called *Passover*. He became the eternal Passover lamb, the sacrifice given, not just for Israel, but for the world. Man had been yearning for an answer to the overwhelming disease of sin that plagued the world. Jesus knew that to become the answer to their prayer, He had to offer pure blood. His offering would be examined by the Church, by the government, by His rival, but especially by God. When the day of testing came, He had to be free from the stain of sin, free from the guile and deception men use to get ahead in life. Jesus had to be a pure human specimen to qualify as the Passover Lamb. Man had lost hope; some had even given up on God.

He was the final solution to the evils of the world, and He would not fail His Father.

How can one man solve the problems of the whole world? The answer is simple. Purity! The world is not ailing from the collapse of its foundational structure. The world is ailing from the core destructible value of sin, and only purity can destroy sin. To destroy the value sin has placed on the head of each soul, now chained to the auction block of death, blood must be sacrificed. Jesus understood the authority of blood to activate spiritual changes. He willingly offered Himself to become the payment needed to purchase souls from hell and death. He was humanity's only hope, the purity of a life not contaminated with sin, and He paid for every sin man would ever commit. Man is now free to walk out of the dark hole of Hell and into life abundant and eternal.

As Jesus sat down to eat His last Passover meal with His disciples, He gave them a commandment. "Do this in remembrance of me." Interpreted, "Continue to honor the Passover by remembering what I am about to accomplish for you. The blood of goats, lambs, and bulls will cease to be, as they are limited in taking away sins. Every man can now enter boldly into the Holy of Holies to converse with God Himself because of My shed blood. Once, and for all, I am giving Myself to the whomsoever at their will. I have consecrated a path for you to walk. It will take you to My Father; it will take you home."

What did Jesus Christ accomplish by being our Passover Lamb? He purchased man from the curse of sin, from the penalty of sin, and the restoration of the spirit of man was made. He gave us the privilege to come into the Presence of God without a middleman or a priest. Jesus made each individual equally important to God, regardless of how greatly they had sinned. Jesus opened the door to God and held it open for us with the gentleness of His love. Those who choose to enter do not have to live under the guilt or shame of the past but are free to enjoy fellowship and audience with a holy God. This opens the doors to life and life more abundantly. Abundant life is life to its fullest, without regrets or skeletons in the closet. Abundant life leads to everlasting life, not reincarnation and its uncertainties, but a life without sorrow, sadness, or death with the Presence of a holy God.

Until the spirit that is estranged from God is reconciled, life is only a frustrated, tormented bundle of bondage in the Earth. Jesus became the bridge to God when He paid for the sins of man. His blood is available to turn the heart to God. A heart that is turned to God begins to seek out the ways of God and begins to follow the teachings of God. A heart that is turned to God falls in love with the Son of God, because Jesus was sent from Heaven to become the broken sacrifice for all people. He was broken by the beatings and the wounding of His body, then He was offered in death by crucifixion as a substitute for all men. Now, no one has to pay for any sin; Jesus paid it all by the sacrifice of Himself to God. He gave Himself as a free will offering to our Father God.

After His resurrection, Jesus went back to Heaven and handed His sacrifice of blood to His Father. This was His greatest accomplishment. He successfully navigated the brutality of Earth and returned to His Father without a blemish of sin. Then He declared, "Anyone who eats My flesh and drinks My blood has eternal life. They will begin to live in Me, and I will live in them. I am empowered to do this because My Father lives in Me, and I live in My Father. Those who desire to become part of this union, I will not refuse." (John 17).

Unity with God is made possible through the blood of Jesus Christ. Those who take part in the covenant of blood, which is a communion with God through the Passover, will become bonded to Christ. The plan God gave to gather His children back to Him after the fall of

Adam in no way has to appeal to or make sense to the minds of humans. God's kingdom is not built on man's approval. All He requires is faith—faith to trust in the Lord with all our hearts. To trust God with our understanding is unwise. Man cannot understand God; therefore, God asks us to trust Him. Trust is the key that unlocks the mysteries of the Holy Spirit, because any other spiritual guide will lead to damnation.

It seems necessary to search out this puzzle and arrange the pieces in order to effect a conclusion that satisfies the soul. That is the solution we apply in the absence of trust. Trust is blind, not dumb. It would be foolish to trust in that which has not been proven. It is senseless to roll over for that which has previously failed. Jesus Christ has never failed. All that He set out to accomplish has been effectively accomplished, surpassing human imagination. Why would He fail now?

Jesus said, *He that eats of this bread will live forever.* (John 6:51).

Perhaps the greatest desire of the human heart is to live forever. In some way or perhaps in some form, we want to continue life. However, the life that Christ offers is not as some wish. If only we could catch a glimpse of the beauty of forever with Christ. We would rise in dimensions of sacred purity and measure up to the riches of His inheritance. When we partake of the body and the blood of Christ, we become as He is and transition from this life into the wealth of the treasure that awaits those who are found in Him.

This is not just a wonderful theory. Many have believed, trusted, rolled over, yielded, and even extended blind faith, yet no such treasure has been found. It is wise not to measure faith on someone else's experience. Faith is measured by our one-on-one time with God. Truth is only found after a disciplined search for God becomes rooted in the word of God. That is the truth we must individually find. It is not a proven concept that catches on like wildfire, which men throng to taste because it worked for the next-door neighbor. This is the ultimate personal experience for our lives as we are found in Christ. God is not on the sales pitch of the century, working tirelessly to gain customers so His kingdom can be proven to be legitimate. Instead, He is sweetly calling us to come to His fountain of life.

The Words I speak unto you are Spirit and life. (St. John 6:63). This is my favorite line in the Bible.

I am humbled to be chosen for the life of Christ to be deposited in me. I await the spiritual awakening that takes place daily as I submit myself to the Spirit of God. My belief no longer rests in the epiphany or euphoria of the moment my desires become reality, but it rests in God. His decisions are wiser and more perfect than my vision. His gift of life is more real than this moment in time. His Presence and heart that beat within me are more absolute than my eyes can fathom. Life becomes a bundle of uncertainty filled with exciting wonder as God unfolds His will in me by His Spirit. That is faith.

To partake of the body and blood of the Lord Jesus Christ, is the outward obedience to the living promise contained in our bodies. Today we accept Jesus Christ as Lord and Savior, not only that we may be spared from the fires of Hell, not only as a guarantor of earthly wealth, nor because we have been handed this concept of religion by our culture. Indeed, today we accept the truth that God has revealed Himself to us because of His great love.

Now, it is time to partake of the body and blood of the Lord Jesus Christ. With full consciousness that our requests are made to the only true God through His Son, the Lord Jesus Christ, we bless the bread and the wine. Just as in the Passover meal, as we pray the blessing on the bread and the wine, they become the body and blood of His Son, the Lord Jesus Christ. We partake joyfully by faith as we celebrate the victory that came because of the Lord's death.

In Matthew's account of Jesus' last Passover with His disciples, *Jesus took bread and wine, blessed them, and gave thanks to His Father. Then He shared the bread and wine with His disciples and told them, "This is My body, this is My blood, a new covenant for the remission of sins."* (Matthew 26:28).

As we partake of the Lord's body and blood in this holy communion, we erase the abominations and the violations of blood. This covenant wipes out destructive repercussions that have taken effect because of our sins, our transgressions, and our iniquities. Partaking of this new covenant lays a new path for our lives. It releases us from the debts of darkness, the promises to fulfill that which we cannot pay, and the blood required at our hands for our involvement in sin. As we join the ranks of holy men and women who dedicate themselves to serving in the kingdom of the Lord Jesus Christ, we lay our signature in blood, the blood of Christ, through holy communion.

It is painted in the realms of the Heavens that we now belong to the company of Christ's saints. Therefore, we surrender to the truth and become servants of the Spirit of the living God so that we may experience His power. Jesus Christ defeated Hell and Death, and now we receive His power to be free from the grip of destructive forces and their effects on our minds and bodies. We are ready to yield our bodies to be buffeted until they are perfected. When the enemy has lost his strength of torment, pain, and temptation, we will rise in Christ over that which subjects man to evil. Then, coming into harmony with Christ's death, we rise to take ground that only the undefeated have conquered.

In the Covenant Communion Passover, we will spend four days with the Lamb of God, Jesus Christ. As we bless the bread and the wine, they become spiritually changed into the body and blood of Christ. The blessing we speak has the power to make the spiritual change. Each time we sit with the bread and the wine, we will commit the troubles we face to the Lord. We whisper our prayers, our pain, and our defeats to the Lord, then bless the bread and the wine and partake. Whatever life hands to us that becomes too difficult to handle, we use the covenant of communion given for the Passover to destroy it. These four days, which we will spend before the Lord, will become a time of cleansing for our lives. Many times, we see the problems that face us, but we do not see the weaknesses to which they are attached. During these four days, the Holy Spirit cleanses, heals, and makes us whole, so we are no longer magnets for the forces of darkness. We allow the tears to flow, our hearts to melt, and the Holy Spirit to be our guide. At the end of this meeting with the Lord, we will be free from the bondage of darkness and made pure through the blood of Jesus Christ.

Let's partake of the covenant of the blood of the Lord Jesus Christ. Follow the steps and the prayers below. Repeat this covenant ritual as often as you are prompted by the Holy Spirit.

Step 1: Prayer of Repentance

God of Abraham, Isaac, and Jacob, You who sent Your Son, Jesus Christ, to die for my sins, I confess this day that I have sinned and come short of the glory of God. I have done evil in Your sight, but with the understanding and knowledge of Your love, I bow in repentance before You. Please forgive me of my sins, take them away, and wash me in the blood of my Lord and Savior, Jesus Christ. Father God, purge me and make me clean. I believe in my heart that You hear me, and despite my many wrongs and failures, You now forgive me because of

Your grace and love. I humbly accept Your forgiveness, and I forgive those who have wronged and hurt me. I ask You this day for a new beginning. I ask that You send angels to minister to me. I ask that You send Your Holy Spirit to guide me and lead me into all truth. I believe that upon confessing my sins and asking You to come and live in my heart, You will. My life will begin anew as I listen to hear Your voice and yield in obedience to Your word. I pray this in the name of my Lord and Savior Jesus Christ. Amen.

Step 2: Holy Spirit's Guidance—Prayer

Dear Jesus Christ, Son of the living God, You made a promise to Your disciples when You were on Earth that they would receive power when the Holy Spirit came upon them. I ask for the power to become a child of the Most High God. I realize that the Holy Spirit is my spiritual guardian as I enter this new life with You. I ask that You fill me with the Holy Spirit so that I may become holy as You are. Lord Jesus, I pray this prayer by faith. Amen.

Step 3: Blessing of the Holy Communion
Passover

Take the meal of wine (juice) and bread, and bless them by saying this prayer:

Father God, I thank You that You hear me. I present this cup to You, and by faith, I ask that You bless it to become the blood of the Lord Jesus Christ. I bless the bread also, in the name of Jesus Christ, to become the broken body of Jesus Christ, my Lord and Savior. I partake of these in faith, believing in and remembering the Lord's death and His blood that was poured out for my life. As I partake, dear Lord, enrich my life with Your Presence and glory, and let Your favor shine upon me. Lead me in the paths of righteousness for Your Name's sake, sanctify and make me clean, and let me be an instrument for the glory of God. Wipe out the plans of Hell against me. Deliver me from evil, and lead me not into temptation. Walk with me, Lord, and instruct me in Your way, because I trust You. I pray this in the name of my Lord and Savior, Jesus Christ. Amen.

Step 4: Four Days of Holy Communion
Passover

Day 1: Morning
Take the cup and the bread to the altar you have prepared for this sacred time.

Read Exodus 12:1–7 and Luke 22:14–32.

Meditation: This is a time of thankfulness to God for the provision of His Son, the Lord Jesus Christ, and His plan for my life. I will reflect on the gift of God's Son and His crucifixion, which provided the shed blood needed to purchase me from the ravages of sin.

Pray: My Father God, thank You for sending Your Son, Jesus Christ, to die for me. Jesus' death was the pardon You provided for my sins. Thank You for opening my ears to hear and my heart to believe Your Word. I receive by faith this truth of salvation and pledge to surrender the rest of my life to Your trust and care. I pray this in the name of my Lord and Savior Jesus Christ. Amen.

Pray the Lord's blessing on the cup and the bread, then eat and drink it all.

Day 1: Noon
Take the cup and the bread to the altar you have prepared for this sacred time.

Read Exodus 12:8–14 and Matthew 16:13–27.

Meditation: Lord, please speak to me so that I will hear and know Your voice. In return, I know that You ask me to deny myself the habits of the past which are contrary to Your holiness. I will reflect on the habits and actions of the past and abandon and reject them.

Pray: Heavenly Father, I have accepted Your sacrifice for my life that was given through Jesus Christ. As I reflect on my past, I ask for a complete washing and cleansing from every involvement in every sin that I have yielded my mind, soul, and body to. I let go, forsake, renounce, cancel, and abandon the deeds and involvement of the past in exchange for the protection, grace, and favor of the blood of the Lord Jesus Christ. I will rid my mind, possessions, and life of any trace of evil because I am committed to the righteousness and cause of Christ. I pray this in the name of my Lord and Savior Jesus Christ. Amen.

Pray the Lord's blessing upon the cup and the bread, then eat and drink all of it.

Day 1: Evening
Take the cup and the bread to the altar you have prepared for this sacred time.

Read Exodus 12:15–20 and Mark 8:27–38.

Meditation: A new life requires new action. What can I do to please the Lord? How can I make a difference that will effect changes and cause Christ's life in me to become a blessing to others?

Pray: Dear Lord, now that I belong to You, will You show me how to please You? I desire to be a blessing in the kingdom of the Lord Jesus Christ. Please take my family under Your care and reveal to them the truth You have revealed to me. Spread Your wings of love over us, and speak the blessings of Your Word into our lives. Cause us to experience the Presence of the Almighty God and desire You in every aspect of our lives. I pray this in the name of my Lord and Savior Jesus Christ. Amen.

Pray the Lord's blessing on the cup and the bread, then eat and drink it all.

Day 2: Morning
Take the cup and the bread to the altar you have prepared for this sacred time.

Read Exodus 12:21–28 and Luke 11:1–36.

Meditation: Blessings will come alive just by asking, seeking, and knocking. I must study and search God's Word to find the blessings and favor of God. It is by gaining wisdom, knowledge, and understanding that I will prosper.

Pray: Holy Father, I have abandoned myself to Your care, being vulnerable and totally dependent on Your Holy Spirit to lead me. However, Lord, my surrender must be nurtured by my study and knowledge of You. Lead me into truth as I begin my journey of finding Your holiness. I will be Your testimony to the world of a life well pleasing to the Almighty and Most High God. I pray this in the name of my Lord and Savior Jesus Christ. Amen.

Pray the Lord's blessing on the cup and the bread, then eat and drink it all.

Day 2: Noon

Take the cup and the bread to the altar you have prepared for this sacred time.

Read Exodus 12:29–36 and John 3:1–21.

Meditation: I am born again because of the covenant of love God has given me. I will sit at the feet of Love, pledge my dedication, and enjoy His blessing. Because I believe in God and His Son, Jesus Christ, the days of guilt and shame are over. My past has no more control over me.

Pray: My Lord and my God, I am truly Yours, and You have accepted me into Your kingdom as Your child. I have begun to experience Your great love. I empty my heart and mind of any residue of guilt from the past, because You have forgiven me and freed me of the past. I accept this gift of life and will increase my worship of You. My Father and Lord, I will begin a life of worship in honor of Your great love. I pray this in the name of my Lord and Savior Jesus Christ. Amen.

Pray the Lord's blessing on the cup and the bread, then eat and drink it all.

Day 2: Evening
Take the cup and the bread to the altar you have prepared for this sacred time.

Read Exodus 12:37–42 and John 15:1–17.

Meditation: The kingdom of God has its foundation in love. As I learn about God, I must embrace this unconditional love for all people. All my life, God has been there, watching over and caring for me, even when I ignored Him.

Pray: Oh Lord, teach me to love; give me a heart of love just like Yours. Remove the thoughts of impurities that present themselves to my mind so that I may be like You. I will keep Your commandments. I pray for the Spirit of Truth, the Comforter, the Holy Spirit, to fill me with the goodness and love of God my Father. Let Your love overwhelm me so that I may naturally pass it on to those around me. I pray this in the name of my Lord and Savior Jesus Christ. Amen.

Pray the Lord's blessing on the cup and the bread, then eat and drink it all.

Day 3: Morning
Take the cup and the bread to the altar you have prepared for this sacred time.

Read Exodus 12:43–51 and Romans 8:1–30.

Meditation: I owe my fleshly desires nothing. I do not have to satisfy my desires. I must tap into the riches and glory of this new life in Christ instead of allowing circumstances to dictate my actions. I must crucify the expectations of my mind and sacrifice them for the excellence of the knowledge of Christ.

Pray: Abba Father, who art in Heaven, holy is Your Name. Your kingdom come, Your will be done on Earth, in my life, as it is in Heaven. Give us this day our daily bread and forgive us our debts as we forgive those who sin against us. Lead us not into temptation, but deliver us from evil, for Yours is the kingdom, the power, and the glory, forever and ever. I pray this in the name of my Lord and Savior Jesus Christ. Amen.

Pray the Lord's blessing on the cup and the bread, then eat and drink it all.

Day 3: Noon
Take the cup and the bread to the altar you have prepared for this sacred time.

Read Genesis 22:1–19 and 1 Peter 1:3–10.

Meditation: The genuineness of my faith will be placed in the fire of God. Greatness is achieved through perseverance. I will never give up on truth; instead, I will hold out until truth wins. I believe in God, His Son the Lord Jesus Christ, and the Presence of the Holy Spirit. I must persevere and be proven pure as gold.

Pray: Heavenly Father, show me how to be strong in the Lord and in the power of His might. I cover my mind with the truth of the Word of God and ask the Holy Spirit to minister the light of God to my soul so that I will not yield to or become a victim of evil. Let not evil triumph over me, but let the greatness of God be my victory. Lord, I give You my life as a living sacrifice, holy and acceptable, for this is my reasonable service. I pray this in the name of my Lord and Savior Jesus Christ. Amen.

Pray the Lord's blessing on the cup and the bread, then eat and drink it all.

Day 3: Evening
Take the cup and the bread to the altar you have prepared for this sacred time.

Read 2 Chronicles 1:1–17 and Matthew 22:37–40.

Meditation: I am loved by God, and I must love God with the same passion that He loves me. In this love is all that I need. To honor God is to truly love Him in word and deed. God will not withhold any good thing from me as I walk in holiness before Him.

Pray: Father God, I am ready to explore the wonder and greatness which You have purposed for my life. As I trust You, I believe with all my heart that You will honor me. Like Solomon, I ask for wisdom, knowledge, and understanding so that I may inherit the full extent of the miracles You have for me. Keep me focused on the reality of Your truth, and let the foolishness of sin fall under my feet. I pray this in the name of my Lord and Savior Jesus Christ. Amen.

Pray the Lord's blessing on the cup and the bread, then eat and drink it all.

Day 4: Morning

Take the cup and the bread to the altar you have prepared for this sacred time.

Read Matthew 8:1–13 and John 6:63.

Meditation: As a child of the Most High God, there are God-given privileges available to me. With confidence and the authority given by the blood of Jesus Christ, I exercise these rights and prophesy my way to victory.

Pray: Dear Lord, let the Spirit of God come alive in me as I speak that which You have placed on my heart. Healing, anointing, a heart after God, salvation, prosperity, love, purity, and joy. For all this and more, I lift my voice, and, by faith, declare these blessings over my life, the lives of my family, and the lives of those You have placed around me. As I speak these blessings, let them be carried on the wings of the angels of God to the throne of God. Breathe the life of God into my words, and let them come alive in the lives of us, your children. I pray this in the name of my Lord and Savior Jesus Christ. Amen.

Pray the Lord's blessing on the cup and the bread, then eat and drink it all.

Day 4: Noon
Take the cup and the bread to the altar you have prepared for this sacred time.

Read 1 Corinthians 11:23–34 and 1 John 4:1–6.

Meditation: The Lord God is holy, and He desires that His children be holy, just as He is holy. I cannot handle the covenant of God while seeking to enjoy the negative deeds of the past. My intentions and my actions must be to attain the purity and truth of Christ.

Pray: Oh Lord and Father, teach me to observe and do all that You have taught me and not to feel overwhelmed by Your standard of holiness. I have the Presence of the Holy Spirit to guide me, especially in times of uncertainty. Release your grace to help me appreciate the beauty of holiness. Help me to understand and apply the teachings and the direction of the Holy Spirit in all my affairs. I want to find joy and fulfillment in serving You. Teach me Your ways, oh Lord, that I may bring joy to Your heart. I ask that I lack nothing but, through patience, become perfect and complete. I pray this in the name of my Lord and Savior Jesus Christ. Amen.

Pray the Lord's blessing on the cup and the bread, then eat and drink it all.

Day 4: Evening

Take the cup and the bread to the altar you have prepared for this sacred time.

Read 1 Corinthians 2:1–16 and Philippians 4:8.

Meditation: One of the gifts presented to me when I accepted the Lord was the mind of Christ. I was given wisdom to think and conduct my affairs as Christ would. I will manage and orchestrate my life and thoughts through the direction of the Holy Spirit.

Step 5: Anointing of the Home

To anoint the side doorposts and top doorposts of your home, take a flask of pure oil and bless it.

Pray: Holy Father, I lift this oil to You and ask that You consecrate it to become the blood of my Lord and Savior, Jesus Christ. I pray this in the name of my Lord and Savior Jesus Christ. Amen.

Take the oil and spread it on the doors and windows of your home and property. This is symbolic of the blood of the slain Lamb of God and protection against the plagues of darkness.

Pray: Heavenly Father, I have continued in and completed these four days of fellowship and communion with You. I have followed the leading of the Holy Spirit. I have meditated on Your Word and in prayer. I have honored this Covenant Communion Passover and trust You by faith to build in me the character of the Lord Jesus Christ. My life is completely submitted in reverence to You, dear Lord, as I have chosen this day. Place Your mark of distinction on my life, because I have honored the sacrifice of Jesus Christ's blood. Grant me the desire to completely surrender to Your love and to Your leadership for the rest of my life. I pray this in the name of my Lord and Savior Jesus Christ. Amen.

Pray the Lord's blessing on the cup and the bread, then eat and drink it all.

16

A Peak into the Future

*Through the precious blood of Jesus Christ,
my future is secure.*

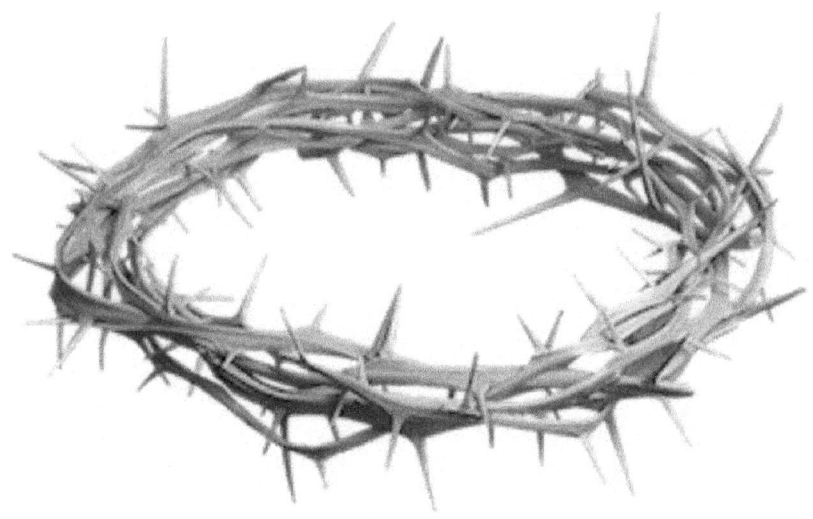

We know that the Scriptures are written for our learning. Therefore, we read them with the utmost diligence so that we may apply wisdom to our decisions. What a tremendous exodus it must have been as a nation became uprooted from a lifetime of bondage. Can you envision the screams of victory and delight, the tears of joy mingled with sadness, the packing, the clamoring, the jumping for joy, and the process of getting ready to leave bondage behind all rolled into over a million people? Can you hear the chatter and feel the excitement of the teenagers as they began their journey to The Promise? The atmosphere must have been charged with hurried delight, because the Spirit of the living God was present. They had invited His Presence in through obedience to a never-before-experienced instruction, and the fruit of their obedience was delightful.

Can you see Joshua's admiration for Moses and Aaron and his desire to attain the success of Moses, propelling him to become Moses' servant? Can you feel Aaron's dream of becoming a priest, serving before the Lord night and day, beginning to surge again? He knew that his vision was becoming a reality. Imagine the little girls who had grown up carrying mortar beginning to giggle and play as they realized that the next day, they would no longer be on the watch for the cruel taskmasters. Old men and women with backs bent, frail, thin, and feeble from the tiring drill of stomping mortar, suddenly surged to life. With a new burst of energy, they straightened their backs, bundled their travel package with the grin of defiance, and began marching to their own beat.

A new day had dawned, and each person was on the edge of what would be, each imagining life as it had never been. This God who had executed a mighty deliverance, was going to be their God, and they would be called His people. All would be well. Provision for food, their own land, their own cities, and homes of their own. With the miracle-working God watching, this was going to be wonderful. Perhaps words cannot adequately describe the movement that led them out; it had to be felt. A mighty hand swept the people together in one accord to pack a lifetime of possessions and be out of sight by morning—the Exodus.

All went well until the first obstacle presented its dilemma. Okay, this was no ordinary obstacle; it was the Red Sea. Visualize it with me. Take two small pebbles; the first is Egypt, and the second is the land of promise. Place them on opposite sides of a long pencil, which we will call the Red Sea. The people were trapped between Egypt and the sea. The sea is about 1,200 miles in length, so it would be impossible to go around quickly. The width of the sea was approximately 190 miles, so they could not even see across to the other side. Surrounding the sea is a mountainous region, and the sound of hooves echoed, chomping furiously, ringing the bell of danger. Pharaoh had changed his mind about allowing his nation-builders to leave town, and his army was in hot pursuit.

What, did Moses suddenly stop hearing from God? Why did he bring us to the Red Sea? Did he not know how to plan an adequate escape route? Wait, was this a trick? Was this just false hope we got through some device or hoax Moses had used to temporarily gain Pharaoh's favor? Moses must have used a spell, and now Pharaoh has awakened from the lull of Moses' trickery to find us gone. One after the other, they began the chorus of complaining questions. Fear was their companion, and they would not be consoled.

Then came the words of defeat: "We should have been left to die in Egypt. We will never survive the horror of Pharaoh's wrath. Were there not enough graves in Egypt?"

Incidentally, this was not the people's first encounter with fear, and each time it reared its ugly head, it produced the same response in these children of God. Before the Exodus, while God was busy preparing to free them from the bondage of Egypt, they were busy bad-mouthing Moses.

"Stop meddling in our affairs, Moses. Every time you open your mouth, life gets harder for us. It is easier for you to leave; we will continue being slaves."

Adversity, viewed through the eyes of fear, can destroy the plans of God; viewed through the lens of faith, it is the process to the promise.

Whose shoes would you have worn in this time of chaos? Those of Moses or those of Joshua? Those of little children with faith or mothers with fear? How about fathers who were about to be robbed of their freedom and stripped of their manhood and their only chance at freedom? Young girls in love who believed they could enjoy the gentleness of a husband were now facing the gloom of going back to the chains of slavery and possibly death. If they returned to Egypt, that would seal their doom for love and family. Young men with the dream of being princes in the camp, leaders of teams, and builders of cities felt their hopes melting like butter as the hooves of horses drew closer. The enemy was closing in, and they could smell vengeance on its breath. Did Moses begin to doubt or question God? How did Moses find the answer to parting the Red Sea in an atmosphere charged with doubt, frustration, and mad chaos?

The enemy can pull a trigger that makes us forget God, forget blind obedience, forget disciplines, and forget the rituals and rites of holy performances. Once we have committed to moving out of the bondage, we must dig our heels in to remain grounded. Before the enemy wakes up to find us gone, we must enter the holy Presence of God, sit a while, commune with and become awed by God. Once we are familiar with the path of entering into the holy place with God, the world and its offerings or chaos have no effect on our faith.

My mother loves the old hymn, *Steal Away, Steal Away*. If God were to lead us beside the still waters all the day long, would there be any need to restore our souls? If the problems and troubles we faced were solved just the way we envisioned, would God's thoughts be higher than or equal to ours? When we tell God how to solve a problem, our ideas are humanly concocted solutions or strategies created from limited imaginations. If God worked within the framework of our imagination, would He be God?

We must allow God to wow us with the wonders of Heaven brought to Earth. God will open the mysteries of secret places with their treasures and break bars of iron as He holds our hands. Our walk of faith must become the testimony of crooked places made straight, gates of brass broken in pieces, and doors opening and closing as we voice the will of God in spiritual warfare. Beyond it all, beyond the chaotic fervor, is a timely truth to be revealed in the Earth. The truth for today is designed to silence the enemy and the one who means harm. Truth will answer the questions of this generation. The questions for generations past are already answered (or partially so), and as the end approaches, more truths must be revealed to parallel the advancement of evil. What if God has chosen us—our lives—to reveal Himself through a given catastrophe? That means the circumstances and challenges will become a raging battle. Then, God will unleash truth and blessings to comfort our hearts, and those truths will destroy the enemy.

Joseph, Abraham's great grandson, was chosen to fulfill the promise of God given to Abraham, and he alone had to bear in his body the scars of fulfilling the promise. His father's love became a cherished memory as his life became wracked with the recurring theme, *forgive*. He had to keep his heart pure and not lose sight of the dream. Joseph had plenty of opportunities to be bitter, lots of people to hold in unforgiveness, and many dark holes in which to bury his dream. We must not bury our dream with the shovel of unforgiveness and keep it guarded with a sour heart.

The effect of the Red Sea, the hot pursuit of Pharaoh's army, and the words of doubt and bitterness stole the sweet Presence of God from the Israelites. Their bitter words became the beginning of the devaluation of the precious covenant they made with God at Passover. The Bible tells of the time of worship after the crossing of the Red Sea but not of repentance. The people raised a storm of bickering and clamoring, spouting words that had the potential to create doom.

Three days after an astoundingly monumental, divine miracle at the Red Sea, where man saw waters obey the spoken word, there was Marah. Marah represents the bitter events that present themselves, not only as mule-buck stubborn, but also with no end in sight. Again, at Marah, the old pattern of solving problems challenged the power and might of their heavenly Father. They did not see or acknowledge God once they saw a problem. They took the brunt of the problem out on the person who was in charge or the person they chose to blame. They had traveled three days and found no water. The people could have gotten down on their knees and given God a chance to perform another *Red Sea*. Instead, they began to gripe and complain.

Yak, yak, yak, until Moses solved their problem. Two months later, the yakking started again. "Would to God we had died in Egypt." Oops, be careful what you ask for! This time, the grumbling was not for what they needed; it was for an unquenchable desire for *bread to the full, and the fleshpots of Egypt*. (Exodus 16:3).

Unbelievable the length of the rope of the sweet nothingness of sin and its ability to yank us back from progress when we begin to enter into our blessings. The noose hangs loosely around the neck and tightens ever so fiercely when it feels its ego has not been stroked. A vivid reminder that it was once in charge. Once in control indeed, but, it calls the bluff, and like slaves, we melt in submission.

One after the other came griping and murmurings and the eventual creation of unbelieving hearts. Could God deliver on His promise? Yes, they believed He could. However, they had developed a system of getting the hand of God to move that angered a holy God. They griped and complained. God supplied. Griped and complained. God supplied. Griped and complained, but God got tired of it.

Moses had to ask God to repent of getting tired or of being weary of His people. God judiciously came up with a solution that honored His Word and, in the same breath, got rid of the rebellion. Children with limited understanding would not be a part of the process, but all those who had disobeyed with knowledgeable responsibility would not enter into this promise. Then the circles began. Some died by plagues, others in war, and a great number wandered in the wilderness until they died, never entering into the land that was promised. (Numbers 14).

Was the first sign of deviation from the plan of God, the sowing of the seed of rebellion because of fear, or was it that they never allowed God to cure their doubting hearts? The enemy, who was determined to keep the children in bondage, crept in at the first opportunity and got them to break the covenant of Passover. All he had to do was get them to speak their own doom. Since he was not able to hold them in bondage as slaves, he had to find another method of keeping them chained. He started by having them spout words of doom at the sight of the Red Sea, and then often enough to weary the Almighty God.

God told His children to keep the Passover yearly as a remembrance of the great deliverance from the bondage of Egypt. It seemed to have become a ritual of remembrance and not a celebration of the covenant of God by blood. How easy it is to become suckered into the cunning of the evil one. When Jesus came, He shared the Passover as a covenant of His blood, not the traditional remembrance, and pronounced it a new covenant. The covenant established on the blood of the Passover could not fulfill the holy law. Somehow, this covenant did not keep God's people from rebellion and the sins that separated them from His holy Presence.

Under the terms of the new covenant through Jesus Christ, we can partake of the Passover supper, not as a ritual but for atonement. Atonement is where the blood of Christ cries out on our behalf. The Father listens because blood is the currency that satisfies the Father's heart. No longer do we have to live with the burns and torture of the seeds sown by the enemy, but instantly, we can be redeemed from the curse of the law through the shed blood of Jesus Christ. In fact, we have an advocate, an intercessor, a lawyer, to maintain the covenant in a perfectly unbroken state. Better still, we are not limited to going to the temple, because He has built the sanctuary, the holy tabernacle, within us. Now we can come boldly to the throne of God's grace in times of need.

We will take charge of our lives and our future through the blood of Jesus Christ our Lord. Life is incomplete if it is only lived in the natural. We must include the Holy Spirit by inviting God's Presence into our existence, and we know that to enter the spirit realm, we need blood. The blood chosen to enter the supernatural realm decides the results obtained and the quality of life we will live here on Earth. The blood of Christ is superior to any other blood. It was shed for access to the heavenly realm, and it is available as we sit at His feet. As we humble ourselves in God's Presence, He reveals truths and strategies that counter the attacks of darkness; we see clearly through His eyes, and victory is inevitable.

17

Treasures Buried In Life's Adversities

*Come unto Me, all you who labor and are heavy laden,
and I will give you rest. Matthew 11:28*

I revisited the story of Jacob, and as I read, I had more questions than ever. Jacob deceptively took his brother's birthright, then ran away for fear of his life. As Jacob journeyed, he found a place where he could rest for the night. I can imagine the man in deep reflection, for now he possessed the rights to his father's inheritance, yet he was on the run. He was a self-made fugitive from the life that had sustained him since birth. This inheritance, which he had stolen, had a death warrant attached to it with the license to strangle the very life out of him. This was a good time to talk with the God of his father.

He took one of the stones from that place and laid it down, and as he rested, he had a dream that a ladder was set on the Earth, with its top reaching to Heaven. Then his eyes were opened, and he saw the angels of God ascending and descending on it. When he awoke, he said, "Surely the Lord is in this place. How awesome is this place!" (Genesis 27–28).

What made it so natural for Jacob to enter into the Presence of the Lord? He built an altar, knelt upon it, and entered the throne room of God as if he walked into an earthly tabernacle. We see an imperfect man who struggled with life, struggled with family, and struggled with God. The story everyone tells is of a man deceiving and scheming his way through life, even from the womb. Life did not want to be kind and yielding to Jacob, but Jacob would not accept the fate he had been dealt and was intent on defeating the secondary status expected of him. He became a man of ingenious designs, taking hold of victories through whatever means necessary, even to the point where he could be labeled a thief. However, throughout his travels, God's divine Presence and blessings never failed to work on his behalf.

Jacob knew secrets about God that we need to know. Failure was reversed to prosperity in the face of adversity, and he used his setbacks as valuable time to increase his profit margin. When Laban changed Jacob's wages ten times and made him work fourteen years for the woman he loved, Jacob labored willingly, seeing a great opportunity to gain more wealth than he had before. Despite all his setbacks, the man continued to prosper. When the time came to reunite with his brother, whom he had defrauded of their father's inheritance, he spent one night in prayer and wrestled with a heavenly being until his request was granted. Jacob did not know how to settle for less than the picture he had painted for his life; it was not part of his nature. He could not see himself defeated; therefore, he was never defeated. Every time life handed him defeat, he looked it over and began planning to defeat it. We see an imperfect man, he saw opportunities to destroy defeat, and defeat was not conquered temporarily, nor did he fight fire with fire. Every obstacle was thoroughly destroyed by the power of the Most High God.

Adversity is the stepping stone to greatness. Moses was born in a time of adversity, when there was death all around. Moses' family were a complaining, murmuring people who were not respected but were used to build the empire of an arrogant ruler. He rose from the rubble of slavery to become a valuable name on the tongue of his family's oppressor. His mother exercised the wisdom of God, and without fear, she allowed him to grow up in the house of the enemy. The plan of God followed, because this baby became a contender for the throne of his threatened executioner. Moses' story is the perfect drama of a twisted tale. The outsider and son of slaves became next in line to rule the superpower of the world. Just before the climax of that incredible story, God foiled Moses' plan and kicked him out of the palace into the wilderness. Another fugitive on the run. His resume read: son of Pharaoh's daughter, successful military strategist, prince of Egypt, murderer on the run. God was now ready to complete the final phase of his God-given purpose. God stamped the resume, *qualified*; he was now ready for his spiritual training.

You must envision a man who was trained in the protocols of the royal palace, trained to command earthly success, now handed off to the angels of Heaven for his spiritual training. God would combine earthly power to rule with divine power to serve. Moses would become transformed; totally saturated with humility and supernatural powers—success to the millionth degree. However, while he was being pelted by the sandstorms of the wilderness, or as he wrapped his coat tighter to shield himself from the bitter cold of the night, could Moses see the glory that lay ahead of him?

To defeat the backhand blows of life, we must become dissatisfied with having someone else always explaining God to us. We have to become tired of the hand-me-downs of who God is or whether we are qualified to enter His presence. No longer can we disconnect our emotions, or our childhood pain, or our social lives from God. God had to rip the ambition of ruling Pharaoh's throne completely out of the realm of possibility before Moses could connect his purpose to God. Then, to break the cycle of the hard-headed attitude, God had to keep Moses in the desert for a while. There is no need for all of that if we just surrender. Moses eventually found the spot, the meeting place where he could be alone with God. Once he found his God-spot, the glory of success began to reign in his heart. This was the man who went up to Mount Sinai to have a face-to-face with God.

And God said, "I will make all My goodness pass before you, and I will proclaim the Name of the Lord before you. You cannot see My face, but while My glory passes by, you shall see My back parts." (Exodus 33:19).

In this quiet place, Moses learned the Name of the Lord, he experienced true goodness, and he found the Presence of God. God became Moses' solution for everything in life. If it was sickness, he turned aside to talk to the Lord: betrayal, talk to the Lord: loneliness, talk to the Lord; God became Moses's rock. Then that became dull, ordinary, boring because their relationship became so real; Moses had to see the face of his friend. His wilderness experience made him dissatisfied with just communing with the unseen God. And there was God, excitedly waiting for the man who was daring enough to ask for a face-to-face. God took Moses on a tour of the beginning, showed him the Spirit of God moving upon void places and commanding light, darkness, waters, and creeping things. He introduced him to His Son, the Word, who was with God, as they took pleasure in creating a world they would enjoy. God replayed the scenes of the first surgery when Adam's rib was being removed and Eve was being molded from clay. He saw Noah and the rainbow, and Abraham and Lot; devout men who, since their first introduction, never erred at being faithful to their God. He saw Joseph in Potiphar's house, resisting sin as a direct honor to his God and his values. He saw the back parts of God, what God had done before his time. He saw the potential of God and the greatness and awesomeness of God, and Moses penned it in the Book of the Covenant.

God needed someone to write about His works, and He found Moses. God was grooming Moses's heart, and when Moses popped the question, God knew He had found the one. Imagine Moses sitting in God's theater as God replayed the majesty of the beginning. Moses' eyes bulging, his heart rate beating on double-time, and his mind exploding with the possibilities of the greatness of his future in God. This moment transformed Moses into the greatest leader of all time.

When we see God, our future becomes history. When we envision the potential of God, we are unlimited. When we dare to ask God for the unthinkable, we capture the span of our lives with past, present, and future obstacles: bottle them, close the lid, and bury them in the sea of forgetfulness. Then we grab ahold of the impossibilities around us and begin molding them through the images of grace. When we find the pleasure that is in God, we do not lament the adversity around us. Adversity, tragedy, bad luck, crisis, childhood trauma—whatever label life wants to use to stomp out our joy—can only be kept alive when there are no secret moments with God.

Jesus said, *"The hand of the betrayer is with me on the table, the table of the Lord."* (Luke 22:21).

Jesus was not bothered by Judas and the betrayal that was brewing. In fact, He let none of the twelve, His closest, know that a betrayer was in their midst. Jesus was not nervous about the crucifixion. He went willingly to the cross, choosing His Father's will over His fleshly desires. These men knew that buried in the adversities of life were treasures that would leave true, untainted legacies, which would ultimately propel the Earth to its culmination. Not legacies that would last a generation or two, but legacies that melded Heaven and Earth together and furthered the heart of God.

Jacob was taught by Isaac and Rebecca to enter into the Holy of Holies as if it were an earthly tabernacle. He was not limited by thought, tradition, or even his sin. Before he went on the warpath to destroy defeat, he locked into the Presence of God to draw on Heaven's power. His brother, Esau, had been handed the firstborn legacy of carrying on the family's inheritance, which included the increase of the physical estate and the covenant of a nation to God. Jacob knew that he who had the covenant had undeniable access and favor with Almighty God. The exchange of the red stew was not an isolated incident; it was an opportunity that was long sought and impeccably timed. Jacob stole the inheritance from his brother and laid to rest the second-best label that was handed to him at birth. Sure, his brother would regret it, but Jacob saw this treasure as worth the trouble. Once the covenant was handed to him, the unlimited abundance and favor with God were his forever.

Jacob walked into God's Presence with boldness, knowing that he was now the heir of the promise God gave to his father Abraham. In his physical body was the promise of a holy God, and God would not deny him access. He learned to enter in and communicate with God as he exercised his rights to this great treasure. In the times he needed counsel or comfort, or through the time he had to serve additionally for the bride he loved, Jacob could have chosen various modes of action or reaction. Instead, we see the unfolding of a unique strategy that made him great in the Earth. His success was inherited through entering into the Presence of God, and blood was the offering he gave for this great privilege. This is the power of blood. He used the blood of the Passover Lamb to measure out an eternal covenant with the Almighty God.

Once we have covered our lives with Christ, we enter into our relationship with God in confidence. Greatness on the Earth is born of those who communicate in the spiritual realm. Let's up the ante. Lasting spiritual success is for those who communicate with the true and living God. We know when the promise is in our physical temple. We know when we have the unique gift, talent, or offering for which the Earth is waiting. We know when the hope of Christ for the world has been deposited in us. To tap into God through Christ is not as glaringly open as we would like it, but the passion of the gift will drive us to cry out at God's feet until He empowers us with the key to open the treasure inside. The Spirit of the Lord awaits our coming, waiting to usher us into the Lord's Presence. Just speak the Word of God and see the Heavens open. Let us take our eyes, ears, and hearts and rip them away from the bitterness of the glitter of the Earth. Saints, the glory is not found on the Earth, it is hidden with the Lord.

18

Authority in Blood

Behold, I come quickly.
Hold fast that which you have,
that no man take your crown. Revelation 3:11

As we reflect on the choices of life here on Earth, we see man acquiring, conquering, building, and enjoying the Earth. However, involvement and choices on a spiritual plane take a bit more than ingenious imagination. There are specific requirements and rules laid down for man to follow regarding the spirit world. Man uses free will to make choices, but those choices are limited to his understanding. As we look at religion, we knit our brows and ask the question, not only with our bodies but also with our hearts. "How can we find the secrets of the spirit world?" Unless provoked, it feels better to ignore the gory details of the unknown, but the trouble is that the unknown arouses our curiosity.

Far beyond curiosity, man has searched out religion to make himself powerful in the Earth. This could be as simple as asking for healing. Religion is really the seeking of help beyond human ability that requires dedication. To benefit from the spirit world, man has to find a god of the spirit whom he can serve and worship. He hopes that the god he finds will bestow on him earthly and spiritual success.

At its core, religion requires worship, it requires devotion, and it requires commitment. Those who spend their time searching out the beyond know that once they enter, they have given up their rights and privileges. The spirit world is demanding, and no one gets to rewrite the rules. Worship and sacrifice are non-negotiable principles which are expected daily. Hence, as man gives himself over to the worship of his chosen god, especially the gods or the God of the spirit realm, he is handed a measure of authority to command supernatural activity on the Earth.

The point is that the spiritual realm is dead without man's involvement. A simple way to state this is that you cannot have a party without friends. Prepare the goodies, plan the activities. and take out the gadgets, but without someone to share these things, the party is dead. It is no wonder God went through the agony of sending His Son, the Lord Jesus Christ, to redeem mankind. God desires our friendship. He has so much love to give. He prepared the toys, created man, then regularly came to enjoy the sweet fellowship His heart desired. After man was tricked into disobedience, God did not give up but persisted in creating an avenue of escape. It is a glorious experience for those who have chosen to enter His courts and fellowship with Him. In this one-on-one time with Him, He lavishes His wonderful, amazing riches, abundant love, and knowledge on them. As His own gain knowledge of this intriguing world and begin to navigate it, we see the amazing effects and wonderful changes in the lives all around.

Blood is the spiritual tool available on Earth to pry open the treasures of the heavenly realm. As blood is shed on the Earth to access these treasures, be sure that a spirit or the Spirit will answer. Think of blood as currency and the treasures as objects available for sale in that realm. A dealer does not deny a purchase from a customer who pays the asking price. Vendors are eager to part with their wares, just like the gifts and treasures of the spirit, where there exists an unlimited warehouse waiting to be tapped into. The goodies, gadgets, and activities are all for sale, waiting to be purchased by those who find them useful.

Lucifer's dark and foreboding curses and spells and all those demonic activities only require blood. They do not require faithfulness, because nothing pure, sacred, or good can satisfy Lucifer. The gifts purchased from him carry within them the painful horrors of darkness and death. No matter how glazed the demonic gifts are with the thrill and dazzle of glamour, at the heart of those gifts reigns death—inescapable death. However, they do require worship. That swindler wants glory. The only thing that keeps evil happy is that its servants show out, show off, and parade their dark treasures for all to see.

"The Blood Will Never Lose Its Power" is a song penned by a famous writer, and it is amazingly true. Jesus' blood is always available to the saints, the children of the Most High God, and its wonder-working, resurrecting power works every time. The sweetest, most tantalizing clause in this contract is that the blood of Jesus Christ our Lord silences the blood spilled for demonic activity. Jesus' blood becomes a covenant for those who use it. They access the blood by prayer, by blessing the bread and the wine in faith. The same process was done at the first Passover: they took an ordinary lamb, but once they blessed it, God dipped His finger of power in the blood.

Fifty days after the ascension of our Lord Jesus Christ, a supernatural outpouring came to live on the Earth—God's Holy Spirit. There was a party in the upper room in Jerusalem where Jesus' disciples were gathered. They were told to pray and wait for the dispatch from Heaven. This heavenly companion would teach them how to acquire greater and greater accomplishments on the Earth. And He came; the Holy Spirit came and filled each soul with the fire of God. As each person tasted of this magnificent infilling, a bit of the life of God was deposited in them. Since that day, the authority of God's Presence has finally rested in the hearts of men.

The Apostle Paul spoke of his visit to the heavenly realm, saying he saw things that were unlawful to utter on the Earth. In many of his writings, he admonished the Church of the living God to walk in the authority that God had given them. By believing in Jesus Christ and His shed blood, the Church is empowered to triumph over evil. *For we wrestle not against flesh and blood.* (Ephesians 6:12). Note that the Scripture refers to obstacles in the earthly realm using the term blood, yet it indicates that to overcome them, our fight takes place in the heavenly realm against rankings of demonic powers.

Consider men who struggle with the will of God and fail, falling into sin. They are not fighting against God; they are fighting with principalities and powers of the dark world. Men who become weak to the demands of sin create spiritual wealth for Lucifer and stage a spiritual competition against God. To win this competitive war, the enemy must break the spirit of man, not just once, but he pummels the heart of man like a punching bag. The continuous breaking and wrestling weaken those lives to bring surrender to darkness. Each person that is broken by evil is set up to pull down the people closest to them, because weakness in one creates frustrated weakness in another.

Leaders have a powerful sway over their followers; it is the law of spiritual authority. Therefore, when the enemy attacks one, he is dead set on destroying all who are connected to the one. The weakness of sin is a spiritual liability that cannot be ignored because it demands payment to the cunning craftiness of the evil one. Weakness can suffocate anyone who is off-guard, and evil only strikes when the victim is down or unprepared. This is how Lucifer sets up his power and authority; this is where evil finds success. The victim does not have to surrender; it just has to be in a compromising position to become a used target.

We can agree that sin is disobedience to God, but God is not duped or overthrown by man's disobedience. God sees the battle, God sees the heart, and God will not allow any man to be suffocated by sin the way His Son was on the cross. Therefore, weakness in man is God's priority. Like Adam, every man wants to hide his weakness, but God knows best, so He comes calling. The authority that God uses to bash in the head of darkness is blood and light. God did it for Adam. The moment God arrived and saw the nakedness of Adam, His firstborn, God covered him. Every time man reaches for the blood of Christ, he is reaching in the Spirit for the power of God's authority to strengthen his weakness.

Every leader is under authority and given great insight into the strategies and designs to build an empire. The greatest authority in leadership comes through accountability. The more a leader answers the details of how he spends his power, the more authority he is given. Ruling over darkness is the first step of faithfulness. After managing, confusing, binding, and subduing evil in the Earth, real authority is to become a living, breathing example of the manifest glory and power of our risen Savior.

There is no greater love than when a man lays down his life for his friend. The laying down of Jesus' life ensured that we have access to God Himself. Now that we are settled in Christ, we can blaze the trail of righteousness through love so that our loved ones and others may follow.

This is not a command, or requirement, or hard-and-fast rule. This is the depth of gratitude for a love we cannot repay. We simply touch the heart of God and pull our hands away to find the pulse of God coursing through our veins. God's authority in the vein of man is the right to control from a heart of love. Through the sanctity of love, man controls his family, his community, his nation, and his mind. In his body, he carries the covenant, and with the covenant comes the power of God. The covenant of promise is not only for a chosen few but for whosoever will, to bring about the pulse of God in the Earth. As we enter the heavenly realm by the Spirit of the Living God, we see our names along with our assignments, and we become unstoppable as we run to gain the prize of the high calling in Christ Jesus our Lord.

19

Successful Prayers

Working Mightly in Prayer. James 5:16

Success must be governed, success must be managed, and success must be built in layers. Success without a backbone is anybody's business because it will bend in any direction. The same is true of the spirit realm. Spiritual success requires specific assignments, specific locations, and specific powers.

The Apostle Paul labels the demons in the domain of Hell as principalities, powers, might, dominion, and spiritual wickedness in high places. Principalities are first in place, time, and rank. The principal spirit of the city of Jericho in the Bible was harlotry. This was the high-ranking spirit that made the city flourish. Before Joshua conquered the city, he cut the power of Rahab; then the walls became paper thin. Powers are spirits that control, influence, or have become masters of human lives. Unlike principalities, which set up their own line of activities, powers must be granted permission before they can rule. Might are the demons that are able to work miraculous signs on Earth. Dominion lords its powers over how one's life is controlled, like a dog on a leash. Spiritual wickedness represents wicked and malicious plots of iniquity and unthinkable evil that stun the Earth and send mankind into shock. (Ephesians 6). Prayer is a face-off with these spirits of Hell.

In the Book of Daniel, an account is given of an angel of God informing Daniel that his prayers had been answered from the first day he began to pray. However, the Prince of Persia, the principality of Persia, withstood the answer in the heavenly realms. To receive answers to his prayers, Daniel had to get the prayers past the blockage set by the demon who controlled the region in which he lived. The account goes on to state that God had to release a fighting angel named Michael to help in the battle. (Daniel 10).

Battles are fought and won by angels in the spirit realm daily. Angels increase their strength and gain victory through the prayers of the saints. God gives the saints authority to change any spiritual atmosphere through the power of prayer. Using the word of God, prayer and intercession are wielded as a spiritual sword. Meaning, prayer has no effect against the destroyer until it is taken from the Word of God.

In this holy place of prayer, man speaks the language of Heaven. Prayer is the ladder of communication which transports the treasures of Heaven into the Earth. Jesus had just returned from an all-night prayer when he met a man plagued with legions of devils. This man lived among the tombs and spent his days crying and cutting himself. Jesus had entered the Heavens all night and returned with the words that brought healing to this helpless man. The Lord's gift of Heaven's language on man's tongue is called prayer. This is the language we use to strangle darkness and bring the peace that heals into our lives.

Peter and John performed the miracle of healing a lame man in the Book of Acts at the hour of prayer. Daniel, who was held in captivity, had angelic visitations at the time of prayer. Though Hannah mourned for years about her barrenness, God chose to answer her cry the day she went to the temple to pray. Indulge me still. As Jesus prepared to face His crucifixion, He went away on a mountain to pray. The Book of Luke records that *as He prayed*, He was transfigured from natural to supernatural: His face began to shine, and His clothes became as white as light. Again, the night before the crucifixion, Jesus went to His favorite spot, the garden of Gethsemane, and prayed until his sweat flowed like drops of blood. Prayer carried Jesus through His greatest trial. Prayer is the vehicle that ushers us into the presence of the Almighty God.

Working mightily in prayer is like making a sword. Words are used to strike, and hammer, and stress the steel until it is worked into the desired shape. There is no giving up until the sword is sleek, sharp, and pointed. Those who understand the power of prayer do not become tired or weary; they wait in prayer until they receive the desired outcome. The Book of James says man works mightily in prayer—not loudly, but steadily with passion and power. Prayer that comes from lingering in the holy place is not a frantic, desperate plea for miracles. It is a secure command of power in full harmony with the Presence of the Lord.

The spirit realm is the greatest trading post that has ever existed and is the standard by which all other stock exchanges operate. The trading post of the spirit operates on the policy of words and the currency of blood. Words that enter the heavenly exchange are called prayers. Using the command of words, cities are built, and kingdoms are set up, but most importantly, lives are traded daily for a spot in eternity. On a deeper, more subtle level, options are issued to secure rare assets. Options are the exchange of values, which results in man becoming owned by the spirits that barter for their lives. Those who are traded on options, have their minds locked in and become puppets of trade.

Unlike earthly stock exchanges, the spirit realm never closes because the business of the eternal has an urgency that mortals cannot fathom. Prayers ascend to the trading floor, competing for answers, while angels and demons have assigned posts to ensure their candidates get the best deals. There are also dispatch services which must meticulously deliver answers into the Earth while protecting their treasures from spiritual bandits and looters.

The spiritual trading post is the economic center of the Heavens used to regulate the economy of the Earth. To be less formal, we shall say change originates at the trading post. Change of one's life, one's health, wealth, and mental status comes from words, and when those words are dipped in blood, change is unstoppable. Unlike the courts of Earth, the post is a negotiating floor, and those who understand the power of words use their words wisely.

Words are used to sound out spiritual laws. Every word that is spoken becomes a spiritual law by which the speaker is guided. That is the power of the tongue. It carries the power of life and death, blessings and curses. When the angel visited Daniel, he told Daniel, "I am here because of the words you were speaking." Therefore, prayers summon angels. The laws of physics can now be introduced into the trade. Positives will cancel negatives, light overpowers darkness, and the strong will master the weak. It is unthinkable to imagine the stock account of a complainer or a pessimist.

The secret to the trading post of the Heavens is to find the most powerful words and bombard the post with them. The most powerful words that exist are the words that come from the mouth of God. They cancel negative words without fail. They are full of light, so they destroy darkness. They contain strength and power and convert everything they touch into beauty. God left a volume of words that contains an answer for any situation man faces. Sending these words frequently up to the trading post is the most effective method of praying.

20

The Business of Christ's Redemption

*If the trumpet gives an uncertain sound,
who shall prepare himself for the battle? 1 Corinthians 14:8*

It is abundantly clear that life does not only begin and end on the Earth; there is a continuation to it all. There is much more to being alive than the physical eye can perceive or the limited mind can process. Getting to know the truths of the Heavens can be a tough challenge. There are so many uncertainties, so many made-up stories, and too many unknowns: it can take the wind out of our sails. This journey needs a special guide, because no one wants to be dead wrong.

The only qualified guide to the Heavens is the Holy Spirit. As we invite Him to come and share our lives, the Holy Spirit breaks open the covenant of the promise. That promise becomes an unbreakable deal that protects us on the journey. Each person who cuts this covenant with the Spirit of God is given a portion of blessings called an inheritance. The inheritance is a measure of heavenly wealth each person needs to successfully live on the Earth. This inheritance package was purchased by the blood of Jesus Christ.

When Jesus bought us from the dark world, He reclaimed the entire package. Each individual born on the Earth is given a package of blessings. Lucifer's business is to disguise himself as a friend and trick men out of fellowship with God and out of the package necessary to live successfully on the Earth. Those who have no knowledge of their package keep riding the donkey of failure and spinning their wheels of fortune. Yet, the same power that ensured victory for Jesus Christ is handed to us in the covenant of promise.

Joshua received his package, fought the battle at Jericho and the city walls crumbled at the sound of his horn. Gideon, the judge of Israel, won his battle with a third of his army, or shall we say, one-third of his potential. The three Hebrew boys stood their ground only to be thrown into the fiery furnace but walked out of the furnace alive with their testimony of faith. There are millions of stories of the lengths God will go to defend His chosen who are paid for with the blood of Christ.

Every living adult can testify that at some point in life, he or she came into the experience of God—undeniable God. The difficulty was to keep that experience of God alive. As a result, we try to regain the experience through other means. But God is not for the superstitious, not available to the thrill seeker, and will not prove Himself upon demand as He has nothing to prove or lose. God is not a gadget on display that money can buy, does not bow to kings and lords, is not summoned by supernatural powers, and certainly is not found by the dead.

God is found by diligent seekers who seek Him with all their hearts. Even though God's expression is everywhere, we must get beyond the expressions and find His heart. We will know we have found God when He sits on the throne of our hearts. We will know His Son, the Lord Jesus Christ, when we have left all to follow Him. Repentance marks the starting point, and faith fuels the search. We will find the joy of His Presence when He becomes our Lord of all. We depend on God because His thoughts are far wiser, His plans are certainly greater, and His vision is more perfect for the path ahead.

God holds the certificate to our birth; He signed our birth certificates as our Heavenly Father. That is why we are called children of God. It gives our Father great joy when we come and talk with Him. He communicates with hearts that are pure, so we approach God honestly, seeking to bond with His heart. It is natural to have questions or to be unsure, even of His existence. God is well aware of our ignorance, so aware that He gives us the option to ask for proof. We can take a spiritual DNA test by asking God to reveal Himself, and He will prove that He is our Heavenly Father. When we ask God to show us His heart, we will find that His heart has been beating with love for us from the very beginning. God's heartbeat of love is full of protection and provision, and He will prove it.

This business of redemption, or the *paid-in-full* guarantor, can only be accessed by truth and faith. Even though God has been there all along battling for us on the sidelines, it takes the act of confession for Him to buy us back from Hell. Sitting in His Presence, love streaming down our faces, lips muttering His praises, God goes to work on our behalf. It is the sweetest experience to hear the voice of God in our hearts as our minds drift toward His tenderness.

Now, our hearts must continue to listen and run after truth. The experience of knowing God comes during times when we are alone and are waiting, listening, wanting to hear Him. We hold onto those experiences by returning to times of quiet devotion. We enter in, focused and intentional, so that we do not lose sight of this important treasures. Wisely, we choose our priorities by setting aside time for this spiritual investment.

Satisfaction of the senses increases in strength with each surrender. However, we do not return to God's Presence asking Him for a repeat of past experiences. Each time we enter to do business with our Lord, we allow His holy Presence to lead us into new experiences. It is the frequency of our time shared with the Lord that produces joy. We shut down the demands of our emotions in exchange for building exciting experiences and new memories with the Lord. The Father of Love has been waiting and has so much to give. Let Him be the guide in this business of owning us.

21

Then Comes the End

*He that overcomes shall inherit all things,
and I will be his God,
and he shall be My son. Revelation 21:7*

This breathtaking opportunity for the discovery of life that continues to amaze us must not control or subdue our intellects. Instead, life must be lived at the pace and standards we set from hearts dedicated to serving the Almighty God. Think of the array of knowledge available today compared to days of old, and we can appreciate that time and seeking are the masters of knowledge. Then the question to be answered is, "Who masters our time so that the seeking may become rewarding?" My husband teaches, "Time cannot be regained or recaptured; use it wisely."

You will agree that only a few have cheated death, and some only temporarily. Time controls our lives, and sooner or later, no matter how long it is postponed, the end will come. The joy is that, after the end, comes the beginning.

Man could search diligently and find the answers of the end of time. The quest for knowledge has solved trillions of matters. Here are two little gems from Proverbs:

The spirit of man is the candle of the Lord. (Proverbs 20:27).

Through desire, a man, having separated himself, seeks and intermeddles with all wisdom. (Proverbs 18:1).

While we are searching out life, we must be careful not to allow the ruthless darts of evil to satisfy or have dominion over our souls. Nothing is more valuable than the soul. At any given moment, a tap on the door of the soul must find it in excellent condition.

To discover who we truly are is to master the game of life. Those who have not mastered the game live in the shadow of the clever or are ruled by the standards of others. We must set our destiny on course and design a plan to rise above the crowd. The crowd follows a blind path; there is no wisdom in that. The kicker is that the search is beyond our capacity of reasoning. That which we can see, touch, taste, and handle has already, in some dimension, been conquered. The things around us do not contain sustainable life, for, given time, they pass on. That which our souls are crying for is the complete and absolute truth. At the end of the finish line, we can look back to correct the errors we made, but then the race is over. It feels like this mystery of life and death could drive one mad just searching for truth.

In His final hours as He hung on the cross for the sins of mankind, Jesus cried out to His father, "Into Your hands I commit my Spirit." At the end, the weight of choice will bear heavily upon our hearts. From our inner beings we will sound the Jesus-cry to our Father God.

"Father, I am ready to come home, ready to see Your face, ready to spend eternity with You." With full knowledge that the end has come and dominion has shifted from man to God, we give God the last words. In that hour as we close this chapter of life, the eternal God and Jesus Christ, His son, will be the names that echo through our eternity.

If you believe with all your heart that your life is truly important, whisper this prayer. "Dear Lord Jesus, son of the Living God and Christ of this world, please come and live in my heart. I truly repent of my rebellious and evil ways that are contrary to Your truth. I invite You to be Lord of my life and to sit on the throne of my heart. I reject and turn away from my past and its darkness. Please, Lord, give me assurance of Your Presence and teach me how to dedicate the rest of my life to You. By faith, I believe You have forgiven me of my sins and violations of Your Word. I claim the born-again experience and will partake of water by baptism, the blood of Jesus Christ, and the promise given to the saints. I dedicate the rest of my life to finding, worshiping, and fulfilling Your will for my life. I am Yours, Father God, through Christ Jesus, now and forevermore. Amen."

www.ingramcontent.com/pod-product-compliance
Lightning Source LLC
Jackson TN
JSHW021901210925
91417JS00005B/40